Honey Sandwiches

From Riches to Rags

Camille Armantrout

As told by

Janice Illo

Friends are family
that last forever.
Love,
Camille

ISBN-10: 1546413974
ISBN-13: 978-1546413974

Dedicated to the men in my life:

To Johnny, for keeping Mom healthy while we worked on this book

To Bobby for sharing his own phone call notes

To Joe for financing the project

To Michael for literary advice and inspiration

To James for encouragement and appreciation

To Bob Armantrout for cheerfully putting up with the process.

Contents

Preface

My mother is a story teller. Her tales of my childhood and that of my five younger brothers have enchanted me for years. At some point, I started paying attention to her childhood. We spoke on the phone every week, and in 2007, I began typing as we talked, capturing the stories and socking them away on my hard drive.

It didn't take long before a three-dimensional portrait emerged. I began asking questions and writing down answers. *What do you remember from the day I was born? What triggered our move from New York to New Jersey? How did your parents meet?*

I ran into surprises that explained aspects of my mom's personality I had never questioned. Eventually, my mother's terminology, phrasing, and the tales themselves, brought my cultural heritage into focus. There was English propriety, the German work ethic, Scotch-Irish independence, Polish hospitality, and Italian loyalty.

Three years ago, I decided to pull the stories together into a book that my mother could pass down to her grand kids and great grands. These stories are as close to verbatim as possible, interjected with some of my own memories and explanatory prose in italics.

MAPS

Janice's World

New York

Ithaca

Elmira

Pennsylvania

Norvelt

Shippensburg

New York City

West Long Branch

NJ

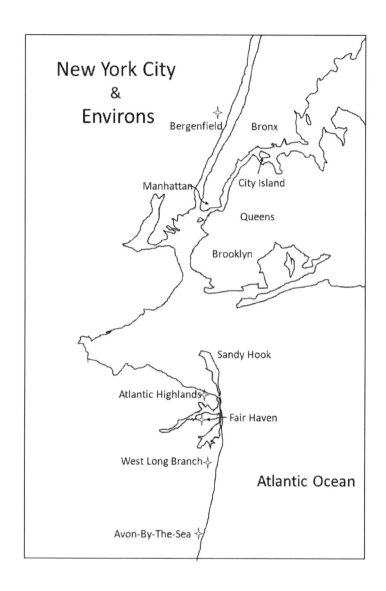

New York City
&
Environs

Bergenfield

Bronx

Manhattan

City Island

Queens

Brooklyn

Sandy Hook

Atlantic Highlands

Fair Haven

West Long Branch

Atlantic Ocean

Avon-By-The-Sea

Maps by Bob Armantrout

Introduction

"You can catch more flies with honey" was one of my mother's signature axioms. It was something her sister told her children as well, and likely a phrase they both heard growing up. I was deep into adulthood before I learned about the honey sandwiches.

The Great Depression shaped my mother as surely as a potter forms a vase. The younger of two daughters, Janice Louise Dunton was an irrepressible extrovert, in love with life, and enchanted by music. She was five years old in 1937 when her father's car dealership went bust, sending the family into a tail spin. My mother refers to it as "when we went from riches to rags."

Mom's parents were forced to sell their home and automobiles and move to a modest house just a block outside of town limits. Her mother went looking for work and found a job across the border in Canada. Against all odds, the following eight years of hardship did little to alter Janice's exuberant, upbeat personality.

Little Janice stayed at the same school after their move, but now, instead of hopping over the schoolyard fence from her own back yard, she had a twenty-minute walk. And a cold walk it was without a winter coat or gloves. There simply was no money to keep a growing girl in warm clothes.

At least they didn't go hungry, quite. They still had flour and crystallized honey. Grandfather Horton was thrifty and Grandma Belle Horton sent a gallon jar of honey every year, so honey sandwiches became a staple. Janice and Jeanette took those sandwiches to school every day. Soon the word "malnutrition" began showing up on my mother's report cards, and her teacher sent notes home chiding her parents for sending her to school with such a paltry lunch. But there wasn't anything else to send. Those honey sandwiches were both a Godsend and a source of embarrassment.

I try to imagine upheaval of this magnitude at such a tender age. It wasn't just the hunger, or the walk to school with her hands under her armpits. There was her father's alcoholism, her mother's disappearance into the work force, and the age difference between Janice and her older sister. When the depression caught up with the Duntons, Janice found herself alone for the first time in her life.

Fortunately, five-year-olds are resilient, and the story ends well, or I wouldn't be here to help tell it. Determined to never be lonely again, Janice vowed to marry into a big Italian family and have six children. And she did.

Some of these stories are dark, yet my mother is sunny and upbeat. She regards the obstacles in her life as "stepping stones to understanding, rather than something dark." Eighty years after her world turned upside down, Mom is still greeting life with an optimistic smile. And her habit of meeting adversity with sweetness has served her well.

This is the story of how one determined little girl survived and thrived on honey sandwiches, love, laughter, music, faith, and family. May her good example enrich the lives of her children, grandchildren, and great grandchildren.

PROLOGUE

Notre Dame Church, New York July 20, 1953
Nell Phalen, John's parents Frank and Helen, John and Janice, Janice's
mother Doris, and her Uncle Emmet and Aunt Mabel Doane

Camille: Tall, willowy Janice Louise Dunton turned a radiant face to John Peter Illo and said "I do," less than a week after her twenty-first birthday. High on the wall behind them stood a remnant of the original Notre Dame chapel built here in Morningside Heights, New York in 1910 - a statue of Our Lady of Lourdes in a replica of the French grotto where she had appeared to Saint Bernadette in 1858. Janice beamed. Her family had just doubled.

Janice yearned for companionship as a young girl, and as she matured, imagined herself marrying into a big

Italian family. Handsome, half-Sicilian John Illo was exactly what she was looking for. She was also smitten with the idea of getting married in the Catholic Church. Although she was still a Protestant, she was studying to become a Catholic. As she walked down the aisle she realized both dreams had just come true.

Here is my mother's account of that unforgettable day:

It was a lovely warm day and we got married in Morningside Heights in the Catholic church of Notre Dame adjacent to the Columbia campus. Two nights before the wedding, I had slept with Aunt Nell in Nana's bed. She told me we were being married on a very special day, the Feast of Saint Ann, who was the mother of the Blessed Virgin Mary. We later learned it was the beginning of the Cuban revolution.

I forgot to bring my wedding ring, and my soon-to-be mother in law, Helen Illo, was "Oh my goodness!" flying around there, trying to keep me calm. My girlfriend, Gail Boker had spent the night with me in the Capital Hotel so she sent Ash, her husband of three months, over to the hotel to look for the ring.

Ashley returned with the ring, and the ceremony began. It was not a nuptial mass, in which the bride and groom are married on the altar because I was not yet a Catholic, but I was delighted to be married in the church at the altar rail as opposed to the rectory. The rule against Catholics marrying non-Catholics in the church had been lifted three months before, soon after Gail and Ash were married in the rectory.

The church was full with John's family, his mother Helen, whom we all referred to as "Nana," and her family, his father Frank Illo, his niece Marguerite Lyons, and my mother, my sister Jeanette, and her husband, Bob Gifford, and other family and friends. My Uncle Emmet Doane gave me away. He was married to my father's sister Mabel, and when my father died, Uncle Emmet told me "I'll be like your father now." John's brother, Frank, stood as his best man, and Gail was my matron of honor.

John's cousin, Tommy Russell was the usher. He was only sixteen at the time, but he looked so mature in his grey three- piece suit. With his pocket watch on a chain in his vest pocket, he could have passed for a twenty-five or thirty-year-old.

Nell Phalen and her husband Jack were there. They were good friends of Frank and Helen from way back. John and his brother Frank had known them as Aunt and Uncle all their lives. Their son, Jacky Phalen, was a little older than John and Frank, and was on his way to becoming a Jesuit Priest.

Mothers of the bride and groom, Doris Dunton and Helen Illo

Bob Tenn, one of John's friends who was on the music team at the Shubert Theater, was planning to sing "I Love You Truly" but couldn't make it, so someone from the church sang the song.

Tommy's brother, Jimmy, was two years younger. He was a kind and generous person. When his father, big Tom, was aging, Jimmy would go over and cook his father's meals.

I remember holding John's finger during the ceremony and he was very happy. John didn't want to wear a wedding ring, so maybe me holding his finger had something to do with him being happy. The tradition of a man wearing a wedding ring was kind of new, and he was not the kind of man who easily welcomes change.

Father Sweeny presided, and Nana was saying he looks like he's just fresh out of the seminary. He was quite young.

We had our reception at the Capital Hotel. My mother didn't have much money. Nana said, "You gotta have some music!" and hired a piano player for $50, which my mother was going to have to pay for. But before we could get out and dance, Frank called for another round of drinks, giving his father, Grandpa Frank Illo time to move his chair out into the middle of the dance floor with his radio to his ear. This was the last straw. My mother fell all to pieces, and went into the bathroom and cried.

My mother had never met the Illos, and didn't know that Grandpa Frank was hard of hearing and never missed a ball game. She thought he was doing that in protest; maybe he didn't want us to dance or something. I followed her into the bathroom and told her, "He always does that, he loves the game. And Frank said he was going to pay for the drinks." So my mother dried up her tears and came back out.

John rushed me out of the reception before family fights might start, but could not find a motel until midnight. We were on our way up to Maine for our honeymoon. The motel in Maine was over a noisy bar. On the way back, we spent the night in the Berkshires near Lenox, Maine, and we stopped to have a picnic at the Wolf Trap, where young Lenny Bernstein was conducting.

Years later, my mother joined us for a visit to Nana and Grandpa's house in Atlantic Highlands, New Jersey. When she saw him sitting in the yard with the radio to his ear, she exclaimed, "Well, he does like to do that!"

The Wedding Reception at the Capital Hotel

Tom Russell Sr. stands at the back of the room.
Back row far left: Ann and William Comiskey (son of Al Kaminski.
Next standing group, third from left Agnes Wallace (wife of Steven Wallace) and Mary Harucki* (wife of Frank Harucki)
Left side of table: Marguerite Lyons (Frank Illo's niece), Sophie Russell (Nana's younger sister, Tom's wife, and John's cousin Tommy's mother) in the white cap with her fingers touching her face, Irene (Wallace) Egidio, arm raised, at the other end of the table.
To Irene's right, Irene E. Lipski, Jane Griguski (maiden name Harucki) standing.
Right side of table: Charlene Kaminski sitting on her father's lap, Charles Kaminski.

*Mary was a World War II "war bride," a woman Frank, a U.S. citizen, met, and married overseas, and who was made a U.S. citizen when they married.

JANICE

Elmira, New York - 1932-1945

I was born July 20th, 1932 at the Arnot Ogden Medical Center in Elmira. My older sister, Jeanette had been born seven years earlier, on January 18th, 1926.

It was a hot day, and the doctor had been at a family reunion and had had a lot to drink. He wasn't really up to the job of bringing a baby into the world. I was a breech birth. My mother just couldn't seem to have me. In those days they put both hands inside the womb and turned the baby around. He did this and it was a trying feat for both him and mother. Anyway the baby came out. That was me.

Grandma said I was black and blue and yellow all over. I had jaundice as babies often do. The doctor put me the oxygen tent and left me there to die. And then he went out and shot himself because he was certain that all that work was going to be for nothing and I was going to die.

~*~

When I was a preschooler, I lived in the rich part of town. We were very well off. My father owned Chevrolet of Elmira. We didn't become poor until I was five years old and they went bankrupt, and then everything changed completely.

~*~

My parents used to let me sip on the foam of their beers. It tasted of malt. Mother allowed it because I went to her first. I don't think I understood or knew about inebriation and alcohol.

Chickens

I was allowed to walk all over on my side of the block but not to cross the street. There was this girl who was older on my side of the block who always wanted me to come in and play with her. She wasn't allowed out of her yard, and she was lonely. I guess she got jealous seeing a younger girl walking up and down the street.

They had a hen house, and she tried to get me down there by tricking me. "Go in there, that's my playhouse" she said, and when I went in, she slammed the door shut behind me.

I was scared to be in there with the chickens flying all over, and I was crying and screaming. At one point, the girl opened the door and asked, "Are you alright?" I said, "Yes," and then she slammed the door closed again.

That's the first time I remember praying. I prayed that someone would come and let me out so I could go home, that everything would be alright, and that the chickens wouldn't eat my legs. When I started praying, I relaxed and then the chickens all settled down, too.

Finally, she opened the door, saying, "Cry baby, cry baby!" and let me out of the chicken house. I didn't care what she called me as long as I got out of there, and I never set foot in her yard again. After that, she tried to make me come and play with her every time I walked past, saying "Oh, I won't do that again," but I just kept on walking.

That was my introduction to chickens, and that was when I learned the power of prayer.

Tomboy

Camille: Janice's father, Roderick, lived in a house with his wife, Doris, and daughters, Jeanette and Janice. Sometimes he would throw up his hands and say, "Females, females; even the dogs are females!" I asked my mother how it felt to be the mother of five sons after growing up in a largely female household. This is her answer:

I felt fine about it, probably because I was always a tomboy. I liked roller skating down the sidewalk from the house and playing with sleds. I remember my father gave me a real sled after observing that what I was playing with was, in his words, "a baby sled."

There was a vacant lot with a slope, and the other kids (it seemed they were all boys) all wanted to use my sled after I got the nice one. Suddenly, I counted. Those boys used to let me use their sleds, and now I was able to return the favor.

One day, I was playing with Bobby Brown, the little boy across the street. He had one of those little red wagons, and I was pushing him. He kept saying "Go faster, go faster!" and I said, "I don't want to go faster, I might fall." But he wore me down, and I pulled him faster against my better judgement. Sure enough, he fell and broke his collar bone.

Ice Cream

I loved ice cream so much as a child, but after my father went bankrupt, we couldn't afford it. For a real treat, my father would get us one pint of ice cream from Elcore (Elmira Corning) for the four of us. He said that tasted the most like what his Uncle Will made at home.

One day, there was an ad over the radio that said "Write fifty words about why war bonds are a good idea and win four quarts!" so I did, and I won it! My mother said I could invite as many friends over as I like, and she'd make sandwiches. Four quarts of ice cream was a big deal.

Polio

Camille: Before the polio vaccine was made available to the public in 1955, polio was a serious threat. This highly contagious virus traveled up the spinal cord, leaving paralysis and death in its wake. The 32nd president of the United States, Franklin Roosevelt was paralyzed from the waist down from polio. When I was in grade school, my classmates and I all sported crater-like scars from our polio vaccinations.

Polio epidemics were common in the summers, and Elmira would be under quarantine. We all had to stay inside and couldn't play with the other kids because it was so contagious. So we made our own walkie talkie by stretching a line between our windows with cans at each end. There were things in the newspaper showing kids how to make a house for themselves in the garage and all kinds of special programs on the radio.

Sometimes, my family would take me to Ithaca, where my father's family lived, because it wasn't quarantined, and we could play outside in the water. Ithaca was thirty-four miles away. It took an hour to get there by car. We didn't have highways back then, so we took the back roads.

From Riches to Rags

When I was five years old, the Great Depression caught up with my father, and his Chevrolet dealership went bankrupt. I was born actually at the height of the depression, but it didn't hit us until five years later.

Before 1937, we lived in a nice house on Durland Avenue in an upper-middle class neighborhood. Our backyard fence separated our yard from the Hendy Avenue Elementary School playground, and I was able to hop over the fence and go back and forth.

My mother didn't have to work, so she stayed at home and met me when I came home after school. She had gone to college and gotten a degree in theater. She met with those students every year in Ithaca. She used to plant carnations and send them to school with me. The teacher loved them.

Mother did like to get out of the house and would take us in the back seat to go sell some fudge to this old couple who had a penny candy store. Not that we needed the money, just for something to do.

My mother had her own car and a cleaning woman, and my father had a limousine. In the limousine was a card table and beneath it a sliding door with a stocked bar and ashtrays.

There was a refrigerated liquor cabinet with Scotch, Bourbon, Seltzer, and anything anybody could want.

After the crash, my father sold our home and bought another one outright, a mile and a half away just outside the city limits on West First Street. It was still a middle-class neighborhood because people owned their own homes, but it was lower middle class.

My father stayed in Elmira to get the house sold, and my mother took me and Jeanette to Saint Petersburg, Florida for a couple of months. On the way down, we spent the night at my Aunt Ibby's (my mother's sister) in Silver Springs, Maryland. They lived there because her husband, Colin Bennion, worked in Washington, DC.

In Saint Petersburg, we stayed with my grandparents George Ingersoll and Isabelle Casler Horton. They spent their winters in Florida and owned an orange grove with kumquats, tangerines, and every kind of citrus. The roads in Saint Petersburg were dirt. My sister went to school in a horse and carriage every morning, but I couldn't go because they didn't have kindergarten in Florida.

We came back to new house in Ithaca. The Hoffman Street School was only three blocks away but our house was not in that school district and we couldn't afford the tuition. That was when I met Ann Howe. Ann lived across the street from my new home, just this side of city limits. Her family was about five houses down, even closer to town. She was adopted. Her family couldn't afford the Hoffman Street School tuition either so she and I used to walk the mile and a half to my old school, the Hendy Avenue School, together. When another neighbor noticed us walking to school, she asked if she could send her daughter Joni with us and save on tuition, too. Once in a while Ann's mother would drive us to school in her car.

From then on, I wore my sister's hand-me-downs. I was tall enough to wear her clothes even though she was thirteen and I was five.

Jeanette as a toddler

My sister Jeanette and I both had under-active thyroids. One day mother took me along to Jeanette's doctor's appointment. She was short and fat and I was tall and skinny. The doctor said, "Well this throws the gene theory all off; all your food goes to waste and all her food goes to her waist." I stuck up for my sister, and he said, "Don't defend her; she needs to put down her knife and fork." But I told him, "I eat far more than she does!" The only time she really slimmed down was when we moved to Ithaca, and she went on a strict diet.

Jeanette was in eighth grade, and every year the eighth graders were let out of class early to sing Christmas carols in the school halls. I was so proud to be her little sister when she came singing down the hall.

Elmira is in the Snow Belt. The winters were so bad that people kept chains on their car tires until spring. The snow just kept piling up. We would run to the window when we heard the bells of the sleigh rides coming down our street.

Jeanette

Jeanette's old winter snow suit didn't fit me so it was a cold walk in my spring coat and a dress with no leggings. I was always tall like my father. He was 6'4" and I grew to be 5'9" as an adult. My mother was 5' 4" and Jeanette grew to 5'3". Although I had a pair of knit mittens, they weren't enough. I'd walk with my hands under my armpits but they still stung from the cold.

Ann wore a snow suit complete with leggings and a little hat that came to a peak. She was so pretty with her rosy cheeks! The Howes were a little better off than we were financially. They didn't have much to spare, but they were able to get Ann a pair of sheepskin mittens. Ann would swap mittens with me until her hands got cold and she would say, "My hands are getting cold now." "Oh, just a minute longer," I would plead before trading mittens.

We had to keep the house at fifty degrees because we couldn't afford any more coal than that. We had radiators and they were very efficient. The water would stay warm in the radiator, not like forced air heat where it turns on and then off.

Janice

The next winter, Mrs. Howe took me and Ann shopping for a snow suit in Elmira. Ann said "Oh boy, I'm gonna get another snow suit!" and her mother said, "No, this one's for Janice." We couldn't find any sheepskin gloves but she picked out some mittens and they were so much warmer.

I felt very lucky that my father didn't send back the snowsuit and mittens like he did the donated clothes we'd gotten before. The school principal had sent a box of clothes home which included a lovely, soft, sweatshirt but my father made me take them all back. He said "We're not going to take charity like that. I can take care of my family."

But my father didn't reject Mrs. Howe's gift of a snow suit for me because he didn't want to tangle with her. He just swallowed it. Ann's mother didn't like his smoking or drinking, and he didn't want to risk further disapproval.

Mrs. Howe was a very strict Christian Scientist with strong opinions, and wouldn't let Ann come over to my house when my father was home. She also wouldn't let Ann go over to the little Jewish girl's house to play because the Jews didn't believe in Christ. Despite her strong convictions, Mrs. Howe was very charitable in the neighborhood, bringing things to anyone who was sick. She brought me books and homemade jelly when I was sick. She always made extra dinner and shared it with her neighbors in need.

I was inspired by Mrs. Howe's kindness, and followed her example as an adult. After we moved to Shippensburg, Pennsylvania, I used to send some of our dinner to our neighbor, Mrs. Clark. Laura Clark received breakfast and dinner from "Meals on Wheels." When she told me she had nothing to eat for lunch, I started sending food over after dinner so she could put it in her refrigerator for lunch the next day.

Baker's Orders

The first year after we moved, my mother started baking to earn a living. She baked these wonderful sticky buns with pecans. I've never tasted anything as good as these since.

They weren't too sugary and had a rich, butter pecan taste. I love butter pecan ice cream and butter almond, too. I still get it; Breyers makes it.

She also baked bread, molasses cookies, and lots of different kinds of fudge: chocolate, vanilla, and penuche. My job was to walk through the neighborhood, taking orders for my mother's baked goods and to deliver them later. I felt so important! Everyone would rave about my mother's cookies and whatnot. I especially loved the ethnic families like the Polish and Italians. They were always so lively with music and someone always carrying a baby.

As hard as the depression was on us, these hard times gave us the opportunity to get to know our neighbors. It was beautiful how we all pulled together.

When mother made bread that had a hole in it, we kept that bread for ourselves instead of selling it. My sister, Jeanette, liked to see if whatever she put on it would fill up the hole. She and my father loved to put gobs of peanut butter, or oleomargarine, on their bread, but I always liked a very little bit of that to go under the honey or jelly.

Honey Sandwiches

"Children of the Great Depression suffered heavily physically, with diseases like malnutrition, but even more suffered mentally, knowing that in a split second, within the blink of an eye, their lives might just change." - (Emily Wang, "The Affect of the Great Depression on Children").

My grandmother Horton gave us a bucket of honey every year, which lasted us nearly all year, and crystallized into a delicious spread. After my father went bankrupt, we didn't have as much money for food, and so we ate a lot of honey sandwiches. My mother would send them with me to school for lunch.

Before she went to bed, my mother liked to dip shredded wheat cereal squares into melted oleomargarine. She'd mix the white margarine with the packet of orange coloring that came with it, to make it look like butter. There used to be a popcorn truck that came around to the movies in town. We loved that popcorn truck because it had so much melted butter. My sister always had money because she was an excellent babysitter.

My dad loved shredded wheat. He'd pour boiling water over it with a little sugar. We didn't have milk (although my mother did keep canned milk on hand for cooking) and we couldn't afford ice cream. That's why my bones are so bad.

On my birthday, I was allowed to have chocolate milk delivered by Houck & Sons in a horse-pulled wagon. This was the only time during the year we had milk delivered to our house. Another dairy, Shoren Stimers, was about half a block down the street, and they had a corn field out back. When my mother baked bread, I'd walk down there and trade some of her bread for sweet corn.

My sister and I were in school together at Hendy Avenue Elementary School for one year before she went to high school. Up until sixth grade, each grade had one room and one teacher who would teach every subject. After that the middle school students in grades six, seven, and eight split out into different classrooms for each subject.

Mr. Lewis taught English at the Hendy Avenue School. When we were studying short stories, he said, "A short story is like a lady's skirt. It has to be short enough to be interesting, and long enough to cover the subject."

And my father thought that was the funniest thing! He wondered what the school principle, Matilda Hoagland, would think if she heard what Mr. Lewis was saying to his students. Matilda Hoagland always wore black and these shoes that middle-aged ladies wore.

During the depression the schools evaluated our health. Malnutrition was a problem and we were evaluated for it. All my report cards said, "Malnutrition." My sister never got that on her report card and she felt bad, as if she had taken food away from me, which of course she didn't. She had already grown her bones by the time we ran out of milk. They had an early morning program at school to help get milk to the students, so if we kids came early before class, we'd get graham crackers and milk.

On top of malnutrition, I had infected tonsils. My father worried about my health. The doctors gave me a big popsicle stick and told me to press it against my tonsils to release the puss, big puss like when you pop a kernel of corn! I didn't realize it smelled so bad to other people. I have my tonsils to thank for my staying out of trouble with the boys.

My tonsils stayed bad until my Aunt Mabel had them taken out after my father died. My father never wanted us to take charity.

The Whiner

During the war, my mother worked at the Remington Rand plant, and my father at The Eclipse Machine Company which had both been changed over to make war materials and machinery. At one point, my mother got a job in Canada as a grocery store demonstrator giving samples of their food to customers. Mother would take the bus to work on Monday and return home for the weekends on Friday. My father drove up to meet her on Friday, saying to me and Jeanette, "We're going to surprise Mommy!" Mother was already on the bus, about to go to sleep, but she saw us, got off the bus, and came home with us.

She always brought things she thought we would like on the weekends. She'd bring me Batman comics but it wasn't my favorite. Later I told her that Superman was my favorite because it was so scientific. My mother brought me some candy one time and I said, "Oh, just a minute; I have to ask Jeanette." Mom laughed and said, "You don't have to ask Jeanette when I'm here, because I'm your mother. Anything I give you is alright. I had told Jeanette not to give you candy during the week."

The only time Jeanette would allow me to eat candy was at the Saturday Matinee from 1:00 p.m. to 3:00 p.m.

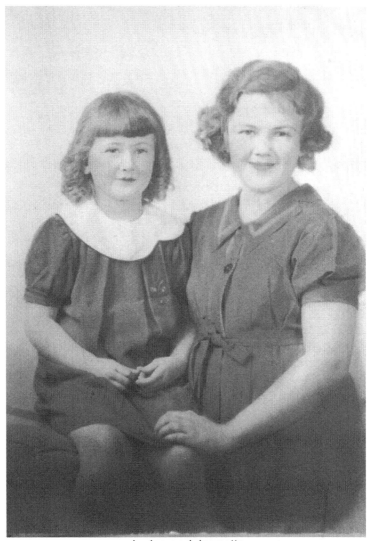

Janice and Jeanette

There was a candy store next to the theater. Jeanette always got the malted milk balls, which were her favorite. They weren't my favorite, but candy was candy at that time. I loved the jellied Spearmint Leaves, Baby Ruths, Mounds Bars, Mallo Cups, and Hershey's with the almonds in it. I liked the orange slices, too. I always liked orange soda. My Cousin Frankie's favorite was chocolate milk duds.

Janice and Jeanette on Jeanette's 80th birthday December 18, 2004

Jeanette had her hands full with me. I was a whiner; I just had to get my way! We were at the fair once and there was this ride, something like crack the whip, which I had been afraid of before, but was determined to ride this time. Jeanette wasn't having any of it but I kept begging to go. Finally she gave in and let me go in but I was scared to death and screaming, "Stop! Stop!" so the operator had to stop the thing and let me off with all these people paying for the ride. Then he had to give all the other customers another ride. My sister was so embarrassed!

Jeanette was also my protector. One night, when we heard what we thought was a burglar in the house, she grabbed a pair of scissors and went downstairs to investigate. Another time, we were walking home when we realized we were being followed by a slow car with several men in it. Jeanette coached me through this scary episode. We tried knocking at several doors where we knew the people, but no one was home, and finally ended up in our own home hiding with the hope they would assume our parents were home. Luckily, they drove on.

Baseball

Joey Shepherd was the thirteen-year-old boy who lived next door. His father played catch with him in their driveway every night. I was only five, but I wanted to get in on that, so I'd stand behind Joey. Whenever he missed the catch, I would run after the ball and throw it back. I just thought that was the greatest thing. That was my beginning of liking baseball.

Ann Howe and I and the other kids would play baseball after supper until we couldn't see any more. Our fathers would stand in the doorways and watch us. I used to play it at school and everywhere. Oh, I loved playing baseball!

One time, Ann and I were playing baseball, (we played even if there were only two of us), and I was up to bat. There was this white dog that just kept hanging around. I didn't know he was there, and I hit him. He was out cold with his eyes wide open and his feet straight up. I don't know if he ever came to or if he died.

Uncle Emmet and I really liked baseball but Aunt Mabel, she liked football better. Sometimes Aunt Mabel and Uncle Emmet took me to the football games, and when we'd go to the games in Philadelphia they'd stop at a restaurant called Bookbinders. It was a fish place and I'd get swordfish. The waitresses knew my Aunt and Uncle by name, so that was special.

My Father's Illness

My father was in and out of the hospital the last three years of his life with nephritis, a kidney disease with a prognosis of nine years. He was also suffering from very high blood pressure. The doctor would give him a hypodermic to bring down his blood pressure. He liked to drink, but turned beet red when he did. He died at the age of forty-one when I was thirteen. The autopsy said bad blood. He drank and it did him in.

At first, he wanted to go to the hospital in Rochester, so my mother went with him. When I was a kid, my mother gave my father a folding recliner that he took everywhere. When he was in the Strong Memorial Hospital in Rochester, she brought that chair, sat in it beside him all day, and slept in it at night.

Eventually, he went into the hospital in Ithaca, so we sold our house in Elmira and moved in with my father's younger sister Mabel and her husband Emmet. I was not quite thirteen.

Sometimes, I had to leave school to take care of my father because his blood pressure was so high. It was touch-and-go the last three years of his life, but there were some wonderful moments. He always wanted us to go to the farm so we'd go, my mother and us. He had to sleep sitting up so we all slept on mattresses downstairs, and Jeanette and I loved it.

One day when I was visiting my father in the hospital, we heard a scream. I didn't know what that was, and my father explained it was a woman giving birth. He said that my mother went through a lot of pain to have me. That was how I found out about my birth.

We all lived out at the farm during his last summer before going into the hospital in Ithaca.

Ithaca, New York

Ithaca was a known for its beauty and famous for silent movie making in the twenties. It was the original Hollywood, which later moved to California. When my father, Roderick Dhu Dunton, was growing up in Ithaca, they were filming the "Perils of Pauline," and he and his brother Frank would go down and work as extras on the set. They each got paid fifty cents a day to be in the mob scenes.

Roderick Dhu Dunton (right) out West with his friend Howard Durbin - 1920

The Pauline movies always involved some poor girl whose landlord was mean. Because there was no talking, they had to exaggerate, so the mean landlord would appear wearing a cape, like a vampire. The landlord was always chasing Pauline because she owed rent, and when he caught her, he'd tie her to the railroad tracks, figuring that would somehow make her pay the rent.

The pianist would trill the keys in a suspenseful manner whenever the caped landlord appeared. Since there was no sound track, every movie house was equipped with a piano, and a pianist would play along with the film, accompanying the action and drama with appropriate music. Coincidentally, Darla Illo's Grandma Scott used to play the piano for the movies.

We lived in Elmira, thirty-four miles away from Ithaca. In those days, it was an hour's drive. My father's mother, Matilda, his sister Mabel, and his brother, Frank, still lived in Ithaca, so we'd drive over on Sundays for dinner. Grandma Matilda was a wonderful cook, probably from having to cook over a fire at the farm. Grandma used to make a delicious chocolate cake using Baker's chocolate and milk she'd let sour overnight. One time the cake fell in the oven, and Uncle Frank loved it so much, that's how she made it after that.

I enjoyed played with my cousin Frankie, my father's brother Frank's son. We cousins always called him Frankie, but the rest of the family called him "Little Frank." Buttermilk Falls was one of my Cousin Frankie's favorite spots. My favorite spot was Enfield Glen, which I liked because the water was so clear.

Mabel and Emmet Doane (my father's sister and her husband) had a cute house on Tioga Street in Ithaca, a short block from their store on Aurora Street. We spent a lot of fun times in this house, especially in the summers.

The Doane's house had little steps leading up to the front door, and a steep roof that came to a little peak, which my Aunt Mabel had covered in copper. She collected pitchers, and put them against the royal blue wallpaper on the walls inside. She loved that color. Mabel also put Tiffany lamps in the two front windows which cast an inviting, warm glow out onto the street. In the middle, on the street side, there was a fireplace and a mantle. And there was a couch against the other wall. Beyond that was the sitting room.

~*~

Uncle Emmet owned Doane's store with a lunch counter, tables, and chairs. They opened at 8:00 a.m. and closed after dinner. They sold ice cream in bulk and cones, cigarettes, newspapers, magazines and knick-knack gifts. They had a juke box with a small dance floor that didn't get used much. People came in for lunch and to listen to music.

Mabel had purchased a four-story building called Pop's Place. She rented the third and fourth floors as rooms. She owned a beauty parlor on the first floor, and what they called a beauty salon (a fitness center with weight machines) on the second floor, the first of a chain of salons.

Aunt Mabel asked Jack Deal, the all-day radio newscaster, to advertise her exercising salon. Ithaca was real proud of their news guy and felt he could have made it big in New York City.

So he advertised it, and when she heard "Grunt and groan with Mabel Doane," she could have killed him. But she didn't stay upset for long because business picked up after he aired the ad.

They also put an ad in the newspaper with a photo of me riding an Exercycle in a white bathing suit and a black mask to protect my identity.

Mabel and Emmet kept the house at eighty degrees, and Emmet was always apologizing to me and my sister for being in his undershirt. My grandmother, Matilda Dunton, lived with Mabel and Emmet. Even though she had arthritis in her knees, she was able to walk until she died at seventy-six. I always admired Uncle Emmet who so willingly took Mabel's mother into his home.

Aunt Mabel called her mother Tillie. She would put her arm around my grandma and say affectionately, "Isn't that right, Tillie?"

Years later, my Aunt Mabel and my Uncle Frank swapped houses. Uncle Frank had this house out on

Trumansburg Road with an antique business. It had a pond and a weeping willow, and Aunt Mabel loved that tree. Uncle Emmet decided he wanted to go into the antique business, and Uncle Frank wanted to run Doane's, so they just switched houses and businesses.

Frankie had good way with people and helped run the store. My Uncle Frank was the businessman and his wife, my Aunt Emma, worked the counter.

At Christmas time, my grandfather Horton always gave every one of his children a big box of citrus fruit from their Florida farm with everything in it: kumquats, grapefruit, tangerines, and oranges.

Grandmother Horton candied all of it. She also made doughnuts that didn't taste like anything you could get at the store. The exception was Burkhart's in Shippensburg, and they only made them on Sundays. We used to stop by after church and get some.

Moving to Ithaca - 1945

We moved to Ithaca after the school year when I was twelve, nearly thirteen. We took the secretary with us. Secretaries have gone out of fashion now, but back then, they served as desk and filing cabinet. Our secretary was a beautiful piece of furniture and ended up going to my sister Jeanette's daughter, Barbara. Aunt Mabel's secretary went to Bobby and Deb Illo after Jeanette passed on in 2014.

Aunt Mabel and Uncle Emmet took us into their house on Tioga Street. My father lived there with us when he wasn't in the hospital. My sister, Jeanette, and I shared a large room with twin beds before I moved to what we all called the cubby hole. It featured a door that opened out onto the steep roof which they had nailed shut to prevent anyone from hurting themselves. After we moved, Jeanette and I went to work in the store a couple of blocks away with Uncle Emmet.

We were on our feet all the time, and we got seed warts on them, something they later called plantar warts. They took X-rays of our feet at one of the Ithaca colleges, maybe at

Cornell, and they could see that it was a seed wart. So, the doctor scraped one of our warts, and all these seeds came out. This was before they knew x-rays could be harmful. They used to x-ray your feet at the shoe store to see how your toes were laid out.

~*~

I started my period at thirteen and had such pain with it that, if I was in school when I got my period, I had to leave. It hurt so much I would vomit. Some people have a really hard time, and Midol didn't do a thing for me. So I was hating being a girl. I was thinking it wasn't fair that we had to go through all of this and men didn't have to.

Around this time, we were studying Shakespeare's Macbeth in English class. It said Lady Macbeth couldn't kill somebody until she became unsexed because her femininity was all bound up with bearing and preserving life. So, she went to the three witches to unsex her.

After hearing that, I was proud and happy to be a girl!

Religion

When we first moved into our new home on West First Street in Elmira, I remember my mother coming up to my room and telling me she was going to start taking me and Jeanette to Sunday School in the heart of Elmira. I was five years old. "But first," she said, "I think you will need to learn the Lord's Prayer." I'll never forget, she looked like a queen, sitting there teaching me the Lord's Prayer. My mother came and sat with me every evening for a week or so until I knew the prayer by heart and was prepared to go to Sunday school.

The first thing they asked me at Sunday school was "Does anyone know the Lord's Prayer?" and I was the only one to raise my hand. I recited it, and the teacher said, "Well, you can see that this girl knows it and that means all of you can know it and I want you all to know it when you come next Sunday."

When we would go to the movies, there was a newsreel before the feature, and there was always a procession with the Pope going into the church. It impressed me, so I asked my mother "What was that?" and she said, "Oh, that's a church." Soon after I started going to Sunday school at Heading Church, we found out about a Methodist Church that was only two blocks away. So, I started walking down to the Methodist Church with two of my friends.

When the other mothers heard about us walking to Sunday school, one of them asked if her children could join us. The group grew until there were about six or eight of us. We had our own little procession!

I loved going to Sunday school. It felt like there were angels in that nice, warm room with the felt board on an easel. The teacher brought the stories to life by sticking felt figures onto the board. When I saw that board, I knew we were going to get a bible story.

When I was about nine, it just came in my mind that we were going to attend the service even though our parents weren't going. (Many Methodists stopped going to church after they were confirmed at age fourteen.) I told my friends, "I don't think it's right that we don't go to church as well."

So, we kids decided to go to the Sunday church service, and in we marched. We were at an age where we giggled easily. Every time someone burped or whatever, it would tickle our funny bones, and we couldn't help it. We promised ourselves we wouldn't laugh, but we couldn't help it. They'd shake their heads and put their fingers up to their lips, but we still couldn't help ourselves. This didn't go unnoticed, so they set us up in the front row where they could keep their eyes on us.

Finally, one Sunday, they chose a college student to take us into the basement during church service and read missionary stories to us. I loved being read to, so this was alright. I had always loved my mother reading to us at night, so much so that I forced myself to stay awake until she finished her housework, which she had to do after work.

That day, I went home and told my mother that I loved these missionary stories as much as bedtime stories and she said, "I never heard of anyone loving missionary stories as much bedtime stories!"

Then the minister decided it wasn't a good thing to take us away from the church, and he let us back into the service. Somehow, after hearing all those missionary stories we were able to contain ourselves. So, it just went on like that until we moved to Ithaca.

When I was six or seven, they started building another church on one corner of the intersection between First and Church Street. My friend Ann and I crossed this street on our way to and from school and were interested in the construction, watching them putting boards down "Bang, bang, bang!"

Ann told her mother and her mother said, "Oh, don't ever go there; the devil's in there!" So Ann told me what her mother had said and I believed her because I trusted that her mother wouldn't lie. Every time we came to that corner we would flee by that place, screaming. So that was kind of funny.

One day after the church was all built and Ann wasn't with me, I saw that the doors were open and beautiful organ music was coming from there. I thought "This doesn't sound like the devil." So I went inside and sat down in a pew, because I just wanted to pray. I had no qualms about it; I just knew that God was present there and that the devil wasn't in that church.

After that Ann would still squeal on her way by the church, and while I still ran with her, I didn't scream any more. Instead, I would look at that church longingly, knowing that God was in there and not the devil.

~*~

We'd get the family together on Christmas Eve and it was quite festive at our house. Jeanette had a lot of girlfriends and her birthday was on the 18th of December so we always set up the tree with her girlfriends. After supper I would join my Sunday school class in singing Christmas Carols to the homebound elderly, and my father was very proud of me. The families would usually invite us in and they'd have a little gift of popcorn or Christmas candy to give to us. I just loved doing that.

After singing to the elderly one Christmas Eve, we had Jeanette's friends over and were listening to my father's music on a big tall radio with a Victrola and a very good speaker, leftover from his rich days. My father would put the records on and sing, and Jeanette and her friends would dance.

~*~

Jeanette used to take me to see all the Zorro movies. I noticed that the girls in the Zorro stories had a little place with candles and a kneeler. I was impressed with that because we didn't have a kneeler or any place special in our home, and I'd never seen anything like that in any of my friends' houses. I asked my mother about that and she said "That's their Catholic faith. They have places to pray." I believe this was the first time I'd ever heard the word "Catholic."

I thought it would be nice to make a little place like I'd seen in the Zorro movies. I made three crosses and made each one a little stand with the larger one in the middle and made it look like Jesus was on the cross. I put them on a little half-moon table in my room with a pillow to kneel on.

When my mother came in and saw it she said, "Why honey, you've made a little shrine here!" "What's a shrine?" I asked, and she told me, and after that, I thought of that as my shrine. I prayed every day there, before I went to bed, or if I was feeling a little lonely, had a decision to make, or was worried about an upcoming math test, because I was alone a lot.

When I visited years later, one of my neighbors said, "Well you got just what you wanted!" "What's that?" I asked and she said, "Six children!" It was true, and I was never lonely again. I was so lonely as a child. I hated coming home to an empty house.

~*~

Right next to the public school was the Catholic school. And someone said, "You have a wonderful seat where you can see the good Catholic kids coming up the stairs." They were always so nice, so respectfully friendly, so polite. When they smiled, it was like sunshine. I can remember feeling that and thinking that. That impressed me a lot.

In Elmira, when I went to Girl Scout Camp, it was very rustic. There were two Catholic sisters who would eat everything put in front of them. They never gossiped or talked bad about anyone. Everyone else was saying, "Ooooh, look at this stuff we have to eat." But they ate it, and I thought, "If they can eat it like that, so can I." Besides, I was thin and needed to eat more. After that I was transformed, and was no longer a picky eater.

~*~

After we moved to Ithaca, Aunt Mabel was very careful to find a Methodist family who could take me to Sunday school each week, and to all the socials. My grandmother would make pepper slaw for me to take to the socials. I enjoyed the different things that went on there as much as I had in Elmira.

One night they had a procession on Moses and they asked me because I was tall. The only way Moses and his people would not be defeated was for him to keep his arms up throughout the whole procession. But my arms got tired, so the others helped me keep them up.

My Father's Death October 11, 1945

My father died in October, soon after my thirteenth birthday. The autopsy said he died of "bad blood," but he also died of nephritis.

I usually went home to Aunt Mabel's on Aurora Street after school and then walked the block down to the store for ice cream with my friends. I loved hot fudge sundaes or vanilla ice cream with pecans and chocolate sauce. Aunt Mabel and Uncle Emmet gave me $1.50 a week, which was unheard of then. Back in Elmira, I made five cents a week. My big allowance came with responsibilities, though. It was understood I would treat my friends to ice cream, too, because it wouldn't look right for me to enjoy things they couldn't afford.

On the day my father died, my Aunt Mabel greeted me and told me the sad news. "Now, don't go up into your room. Your father would want you to live your life as you do, so go on out and get some ice cream with your friends." So I went, but I was biting my tongue all the time. When my Uncle Emmet heard me talking with all my friends just like I always did, he asked, "Did you go home yet?" "Yes," I told him, and he just shrugged his shoulders because he couldn't understand why I was acting like nothing had happened.

Janice, her father, and Tiana

So, I kept everything inside until one day when I was staying with my girlfriend Barbara Jones. She was the kind of person I could reflect with. We were best friends in Elmira as eleven-year-olds. Her mother was the scout den mother. They moved away when she was twelve. I was invited to go down there for two weeks right around my fourteenth birthday. We stayed awake at night talking about everything. She asked me about my father, and I just started bawling. I started talking and talking and crying, but it was the most wonderful outlet for me to open up about my father. They asked, "Are you alright?" "Yes, I am," I told them, and I really felt good after that.

Our Boston Bull Terrier, Tiana, died that year, too. She was fourteen, a year older than I.

Doane's Store

Later that year, my mother, sister, and I moved into the rooms above Doane's Store. There was a railing, really pretty, with ornate lights at each end, which led back to the door to an apartment upstairs. Aunt Mabel had it built and put a nice tree out there, too.

Bob Gifford and his four war buddies roomed around the corner. They came into the store at night where my sister Jeanette and I worked behind the counter. Jeanette was paid, but I had to work for free until I turned fourteen and got my working papers. Bob was always kidding around, was always big at talking to waitresses and making everybody laugh.

Bob lived with us while he got his master's degree in Physical Education. We had two beds in the bedroom, and he slept out in the living room.

The teens hung out there at the store. They'd sit on the railing, and when Bob Gifford would come around (he was courting my sister Jeanette), he would say, "Hello, men!" And they'd talk and talk and then he'd say, "Well, I gotta go see the lady upstairs."

The Sugar Bowl

My mother and I decided we were ready to branch out on our own, so we bought a little luncheonette called The Sugar Bowl in downtown Ithaca when I was sixteen. Mother and I each put in $1400 for the down payment and bought it from the people who owned the bar on the other side.

When my father died, he left his Social Security. He didn't have any saved money or anything. My sister Jeanette and I each got $1,400, and my mother got $3,000. So, when we were looking for a store and wanted to buy the Sugar Bowl, I pitched in my share, and we both signed papers. Jeanette was in Elmira College and able to get a real good job up at Cornell in administration, so she didn't need to throw in with us.

We were still living above Doane's, so we took the bus to the Sugar Bowl. We later rented an apartment within walking distance on South Hill. It was a real cheapy, built on the side of a hill, with just a little patch of grass and a short sidewalk. They were what you call shotgun apartments, basically a long hallway with apartments along the hall, the narrow end facing the road.

The Sugar Bowl was a place people could come and sit all day, folks without much money who just wanted to hang around. A woman once told me, "Your mother has a gift; she is so wonderful to be with."

We served sandwiches and milkshakes, and we had weekday specials. One day it would be spaghetti and meatballs, and on another it would be chicken cooked a long time with vegetables. I liked just a little bit of chocolate in my milkshakes. We pretty much served the same things they served at Doane's. It was right in the center of town. We served coffee and pie my mother bought from the pie lady.

We opened The Sugar Bowl daily from 6:30 a.m. until the movies started at 7:00 p.m. Then mother and I would walk to the movies half a block away to catch some sleep in the theater. My mother's internal alarm clock would always go off at 8:30 in time for her to wake me up and walk back to the store to reopen at 9:00 when the movies let out. Once it cleared out we'd go back to the movies for the second feature, take another cat nap, then reopen again for the second round of after-movie patrons.

Around 2:00 p.m., after the lunch crowd, mother would go to one of the back booths and rest her head on the table for a nap. Sometimes she'd catch a nap in the chair she had given my father. She had slept beside him in that chair at the hospital in Rochester. My mother kept the chair in the tiny bathroom at the Sugar Bowl.

When my friend Maggie Rich came into the Sugar Bowl she asked, "What's this on the spindle, all these notes, 'be back at such and such a time' for so many different times; when are you ever open?"

Eventually we moved down off of South Hill to live above the Sugar Bowl, so my mother stopped buying pies from the pie lady and started baking her own.

My mother could make a pie in fifteen minutes, with me there to watch the counter. And they were delicious; so tender and crispy. She never could figure out why it took me so long to make pies. I made a cherry pie for Valentine's Day, and it took me three hours. Mother said, "Well I never heard of anyone taking that long to make a pie."

By now she was exasperated, and she wanted to hurry up and get on to the next thing. So I stuck up for myself and said, "Well, I'm new at it." But years of experience only helped speed me up a little. It still takes me two hours to make a pie.

Later, we moved to a two-room apartment above the Sugar Bowl, and there was a hall and stairs that went between the bar and restaurant. Years later, when I'd bring Camille and Johnny for a visit, mother would sleep in the living room and give us her room. I had my bell collection in the apartment. I'd been collecting bells since high school. That was Camille and Johnny's main joy, playing with those bells.

There was a beer parlor on the other side of the Sugar Bowl. We each had a juke box, but the music played on both sides, so there was a crazy mix of tunes, some of them pretty wild. I was amused by the hair-raising, tear-dropping songs from the bar next door.

Here's an example of a song they would play on the jukebox next door:

Don't roll those bloodshot eyes at me
I can see you've been out on a spree
....

Your eyes look like two cherries in a glass of buttermilk
Don't roll your bloodshot eyes at me

And then there was:

You are my sunshine, my only sunshine
You make me happy when skies are gray...

I used to go out and pay the rent next door. And when I'd walk into the bar with some of those songs playing, I'd see tears coming out of the eyes of the men in the booths. I hated going in there because the men were all over me, but they never hurt me or anything.

My mother had kept the chair she'd given my father; the one that she slept in beside him when he was in the hospital, and she put it in the bathroom at the Sugar Bowl. When it got slow, she would take a little nap in that chair in the bathroom.

When I was taking care of the Sugar Bowl by myself one day, a man came by and asked to see the manager. I thought he said "the men's room," so I pointed in the direction of the bathroom. He came out and asked me again, and again I was sure he said "the men's room." So I said, "Well, there's only one!" and he went back there and said, "Well, you still don't understand." Technically, I was the manager because my mother and I were co-owners. But I didn't even think to tell him that I was manager. I just got red in the face.

Cascadilla School

I remember everyone said how organized Uncle Emmet was. He'd say, modestly, "That's because I'm naturally so disorganized!" Emmet was a smart man, and he offered to teach me physics. He was trying to teach it to me, but I wasn't learning it because I wasn't good at math. I didn't take algebra in school.

I majored in language and studied Spanish because I wanted to go to South America. This was my father's dream, too. He introduced me to South American music, and we both loved it. He used to play Ravel's "Bolero" for me. He liked Xavier Cugat, but I thought he was too Americanized. That's as close as we got to popular music. I liked Desi Arnaz, Lucille Ball's husband, because he played the real stuff: "Baloo, babaloo."

I went to Ithaca High School my freshman year and Joan Schaltzaur was one of my best friends. She had two younger brothers. I studied French that year because they didn't offer Spanish. I was able to take Spanish at Cascadilla School, the college preparatory school in Cornell, during my last three years of high school.

Joan's family spent their summers at the yacht club, and I was able to join them as their guest those years I was at Cascadilla. Mrs. Schaltzaur loved to rough it, camping and cooking outdoors at one of the cottages at the yacht club. Joan's family was well off and could afford to send her to Cornell. But I never made it to Cornell because we couldn't afford the tuition.

Concert Pianist

Back when I was two or three years old, my mother got a Kimball upright standard piano so we could learn to play. My favorite brand was Chickering. To me, it had the best sound of any piano. I never was very fond of Steinway, but Steinway was very popular.

My sister Jeanette wanted to play guitar, so she never bothered with the piano, but little me, I walked over there and started plunking the notes. There was one note, a low note that had such resonance, I can still hear it! Jeanette said, "Mother, make her stop!" but Mother said, "I bought that piano here to be played, and you're not playing it, but she is."

So I played that Kimball. That was what I plunked around on. When I was five and we moved to West First Street, we took the piano with us. There was a little porch which was to become my play room, and we put the piano along with things to paint and color with in there.

I just played all the time, and I'm sure my mother and Jeanette might have been irritated, but my mother never said anything to discourage me. Boogie woogie sounded a little blah to me (da da da dum), so I added another beat in between the notes: da da, da da, da da, dum, and then I added a top line melody. So my right hand was really going and my left hand, too. Playing the piano was my main pastime because I was alone a lot.

Then I started making up my own tunes. I wanted to be a concert pianist and composer when I grew up. It got easier and easier, and once in a while, I could just sit down and play something simply and easily.

My father was first hospitalized with nephritis soon after going bankrupt. He wanted to give me piano lessons, but was in and out of hospitals and didn't have enough money for lessons. In fact, we were really poor. They had to give me free meals at school because I wasn't getting enough to eat.

So, I'd go to Ann Howe's when she took her lesson and sit outside her house and listen. Then I'd go back home and try to figure it out, though I wasn't great like some people who don't even have to try.

When my father would come home from the hospital to recover, I'd try not to play so much. But when I stopped playing he asked, "Why did you stop?" And I said, "Well I thought it might disturb you," and he said "Ah, don't ever stop, I love to hear it!" He was just so encouraging to me. He loved music too, and would say; "Okay, let's have our concert," meaning "Let's play our records," like Tchaikovsky.

Music was big with the people back then before TV. Every house had a piano and there were dozens of piano manufacturers in the U.S.

As I got older, he got worse and worse. Then, when he was real ill and had to go to hospital for good, he wanted to stay in the Ithaca hospital so his mother and Aunt Mabel could visit him. My mother, sister, and I didn't move to Ithaca until after I was finished with the school year. We went to live with my Aunt Mabel, leaving the Kimball behind in Elmira. I remember hearing that we sold the house for $700.

Cousin Maud and Aunt Mabel pooled their money and got me a baby upright piano, a Culbertson, and Aunt Mabel got Mr. Bardwell to give me music lessons. He was the Lutheran church organist and the best music teacher in town. Lessons with Mr. Bardwell were $3 an hour, which was very expensive at that time. The other piano teachers charged $1 an hour.

Well, of course by then, I was playing things like Chopin and so on by ear, so to go back and learn how to read notes took willpower. It was alright though; I had the willpower because I wanted to learn to read music very badly. One of my friends, Carolyn Bailey, who lived a block from Aunt Mabel's, knew how to read music and played beautifully. She was even able to improvise. Her family had custom-built their home, and they had two pianos, one of them a Steinway.

Aunt Mabel was good to try and make things work out after my father died, but every time I took a lesson, I thought of him so much I cried. I thought about how much he had wanted me to have lessons but couldn't afford them and how unfortunate it was that he wasn't here to see me finally getting to take them. Later, when I converted to the Catholic Church, I learned that he would have known about my lessons. They taught me that your loved ones can see you from up in heaven. But, at the time, I didn't know this, and it was breaking my heart.

So, I just cried every time I had a piano lesson because my father wasn't here to see it. Finally after six months, I said, "I just can't do it anymore," and Mr. Bardwell said, "What did I do, what did I say? I need to know so I can stop it." "No, no; it's not you," I said and told him about my father. I assured Aunt Mabel that I would take lessons again, and I did try a few times, but ended up being satisfied with just being able to hear it and play. I'd go down to Carolyn's and listen to her, and then I'd play it, too. She couldn't believe I could do that.

And I loved to harmonize. We'd sit around in the evening and sing, and I'd join them and harmonize with them. And that is in me, the notion of two notes together making another sound. And there was another thing. I couldn't whistle, but my father could. He had a good voice for singing and he was a wonderful whistler. He could whistle two notes at the same time and he tried to teach me.

When I was in high school, I met Miss Bryant who had been there when my father was in the high school glee club. When she heard I was his daughter she wanted to talk to me. She was a character, and had been written up in Reader's Digest.

Miss Bryant imagined that I could do anything. She asked me if I played, and I said "Yes, I can play," so she said, "I want to hear you." She just got it in her head that I could play anything. She wanted me to get a scholarship. But, I couldn't play as fast as that.

There was this girl who played well. She was one of the "Hill Kids" who were rich, but because they were well off, they toed the line. They were very good, very nice people. I loved what she played and went back and learned a lot of things just from hearing her. She played as the people came in for the weekly school assembly, to get them in the mood and, again, as the people left the auditorium.

There was a contest every Friday afternoon as part of the assembly. The school thought it would be nice to get a second pianist, so they used the contest to choose one. I entered the contest and thought, "Well, I'm going to do something that no one else does and I'm going to win it." I made up my own concerto in three different movements and played part or all of it.

So, they took a vote via a raise of hands and I won it hands down. I got it! I remember this boy who was popular and in sports and all. He said, "Dunton, that was great; I didn't know you could do that." So, I was feeling really good and, from then on, I played for the assembly every Friday.

Mr. Bardwell told me in passing, because he knew my aspiration was to be a concert pianist and composer, that I would make a fine composer, but my double-jointed thumbs were a problem when it came to being a concert pianist because there was no power in them. These thumbs of mine! What I had to do if I wanted to play something fast was to use my fingers to compensate for my thumbs. I could fake it, you know, but it wouldn't be anything for a concert stage.

That was my zenith as far as music went.

My son, Michael, also has this ability to hear and play music. He started playing the piano when we lived out at the farm in 1975. I noticed he made up songs. He even wrote a song called "Lady Wisdom" based on the bible.

Michael playing a fife

Camille: Michael can pick up and create magic with any kind of musical instrument. His collection includes guitars, fiddles, fifes, flutes, and a piano.

I couldn't wait to be a Brownie Scout. I was lonely at home because my mother had to work, and Jeanette was always babysitting. So, I became a Brownie, and that's how I met Shirley Schaefer, a friend of Ann Howe's. During Scout meetings, Shirley would play around on the piano, so I'd go over there. I loved the way she played The New World Symphony by Antonín Dvořák, and so, one day, I told her I'd learned it. She wanted to hear me play it, so did, and she couldn't get over how much it sounded like what she was playing. I believe Shirley did go on to become a concert pianist.

My Indian

When I was sixteen I bought myself a motorcycle, an Indian Arrow, in my favorite color: robin's egg blue. It was the first year Indian made the small Arrow model. It only held one gallon of gas.

I didn't want to drive a car because I'd always gotten car sick. You could get a driver's permit when you turned fourteen and a license at sixteen. Even though I had never driven a motorcycle, I'd ridden on them, and I was used to seeing people pull up to Doane's Store on motorcycles.

The motorcycle shop was only half a block away from Doane's and there was this history professor who had part ownership in the motorcycle shop and taught up at Cornell. He'd ride his motorcycle to the store and when I saw him I thought, "That's the answer."

So, my mother brought a blazer and a kerchief to work one day, and when the professor showed up, she asked him to give her a ride on his motorcycle so she could decide if it was safe enough for her daughter. Jeanette was mortified and thought Mother was being a terrible mom. But my mother decided they were very safe and gave me permission to buy one.

I got permission from my mother to use some of the trust fund money my grandfather had left me for a down payment. I used my pay from working weekends at Doane's Store to make the payments, and kept the money I made working after school for pocket money. In August, I'd go shopping for school clothes at the Sears and Roebuck in Courtland.

One night my friend Maggie and I took my motorcycle and went out drinking at Lansing Inn. I hated that place. We saw a woman who must have been ninety, she was so wrinkled, playing cards with this man who looked about fifty years old. Every once in a while he'd kiss her and we thought, "Ewww!"

I don't know how we even got home, and my mom was out in her nightgown waiting for us in front of Aunt Mabel's store. Maggie said, "Boy she's mad to come right out of doors and not think about what the neighbors think."

There was another night when I told my mother I was going out with the motorcycle club. This time I rode on the back of one of the other bikes. It was real cold, but I didn't like the guy that I rode with, so I wouldn't hold on and get warm. I should have dressed warmer. I didn't even bring a sweater! But we girls huddled together after we got off the bikes.

We all stopped at this diner in town (it might have been my Cousin Frank's) and got these tuna fish salad sandwiches and some hot chocolate, which warmed us right up. This time, my mother knew when to expect me home and didn't have to wait outside on the porch for me.

I was a little more free because I didn't have a father. I remember feeling that, if my father were alive; I wouldn't be able to be out late at night. I was glad I didn't have that restraint, and I felt terrible about having that feeling so I told my mother. And she said, "We all feel that way at your age but that passes."

Jeanette didn't approve of me having a motorcycle at that age. She hated it, even though my mother didn't seem concerned. "My sister rode to the State Fair and didn't get home until 2:00 a.m.!" she told Camille.

My cousin, Bobby Zimmer, lived in Syracuse, about an hour and a half away, and I liked to go up there to visit him on my motorcycle. I was up there one time when a newspaper reporter saw me. I was riding my Indian up this hill with the wind blowing my hair and he wanted to take a picture of me for the paper. I kept running away from him until he jumped out of his car at the light and showed me his identification.

Camille: On June 11, 1950, "The Post-Standard" newspaper out of Syracuse, New York ran the following story:

"Miss Dunton, Ithaca Sr., Often Clips Off 300 Miles Just Riding' Own Motorcycle

"Miss Janice Dunton 17-year-old Ithaca high school Sr., and daughter of Mrs. Doris Dunton, 1005 N. Aurora St. has an unusual avocation, for a girl.

"She is a motorcycle enthusiast, owns and drives her own lightweight model machine.

"Ithaca has many motorcyclists, predominantly men. It's hard to state accurately whether Miss Dunton is the only girl who owns and drives her own motorcycle here, but she rides it more frequently than any, if there are others, and tho it never ceases to be an unusual sight, she is commonly seen flitting about city streets aboard her trusty iron steed.

"Janice has been interested in motorcycles since she was a little girl, principally because there formerly was a motorcycle shop near her home and she always heard the machines roaring and saw people riding them. She started riding behind others when she was 14, and began driving herself when she purchased her 'cycle about a year ago. She took the customary spills while learning to negotiate the motorcycle and today is considered an accomplished driver.

"Sufficiently accomplished in fact that now she is itching to own and ride a heavier machine, Something with a little more pickup and snap," as she explains it.

"Oddly enough, Miss Dunton, now at an age when most girls are "simply wild about cars," has little enthusiasm for riding in or driving an automobile.

"'You can get places with a motorcycle that you can't with a car,' she says, pointing out she has never even particularly liked riding in a car. One thing she likes about motorcycle riding is, "the wind in my face."

THE POST-STANDARD 27

Miss Dunton, Ithaca Senior, Often Clips Off 300 Miles Just Riding Own Motorcycle

"Janice has always been an out-of-doors type of girl, liking to hike and spends as much time as possible in the open air. She gets plenty of it with the cycle. Tho never having taken any long trips-

Syracuse is about as far away from home as she has strayed with the machine-she often puts 300 miles a day on the speedometer, "just cruising around."

"She spends as much time as possible every day riding, even motoring to school and parking her 'cycle in the racks beside the high school. It's the only motorcycle ridden by a girl there, and as far as she knows, by a boy either.

"Several motorbikes are parked about the high school, ridden by boy students. These are motorized versions of a bicycle and not comparable to the machine she rides, which is capable of "winding up" to 80 miles an hour, tho naturally she doesn't ride it that fast.

"Janice definitely has something her classmates don't have, and she is the center of attraction each school day as she arrives aboard the cycle and "buzzes" home quickly when classes are over. Frequently she gives friends a ride, double, and Ithacans yet haven't quite got used to seeing a pair of girls flitting about on a motorcycle, with one of them at the controls."

My Brother-in-Law, Bob Gifford

When Jeanette and I first met Bob Gifford he was studying physical education because he wanted to be a coach. And he went on to coach and inspire many people over his long career. He and Jeanette married in October of 1948, so he was a part of the family for fifty years. He died in 1998.

Bob Gifford (we called him Giff) was like a big brother to me. He was nine years older than Jeanette, which made him sixteen years older than me. He came into my life when I was only thirteen, shortly after my father died. He saw my need to be active, and agreed to teach me how to play ping pong. I had been the first one in my gym class to 'fail' ping pong and really wanted to learn.

Uncle Emmet let us use a table he had in the store. It was nicked up, and he was going to throw it out. Giff taught me to play so well! I learned forehand, backhand and how to put spin on the ball when I served it. He taught me how to wait a split second to see where the ball was going after the bounce so I was able to return it. And with my backhand, I was able to return their forehand slams. He taught me how to tip the paddle so that the ball would go just over the net.

Jeanette and Bob Gifford's wedding
Standing: Doris Dunton, Janice, Jeanette, Bob Gifford, Giff's best man,
Mabel, and Emmet Doane.
Seated: Isabelle Horton and Matilda Dunton

Whereas before I used to hit them way up in the sky! I'd hit them up into the ceiling! The upshot was, I was able to join the high school ping pong club as a sophomore. Every year they had a competition and I played so well, I won the championship against juniors and seniors that first year, and every year after!

Then I was able go out and join Club 202 at the YMCA. They had three different rooms. One was for dancing and they had an elderly couple in there as chaperones if you wanted to dance. Another room had cards, chess and checkers. And the third room had shuffleboard and ping pong. Naturally, I headed right to the ping pong room!

When I'd come back at night, Bob and Jeanette would be sitting in the living room with their friends. They were enthralled at how enlivened I was. It was so good to be empowered by ping pong. I had been kind of mousy after my father's death, not loquacious like I was when I'd come back from ping pong at Club 202!

Giff said, get your girlfriends together, and I'll teach you how to play tennis. And he was so good with everyone, showing each individual how to hold their racket, how to keep their eye on the ball, and the way they should position themselves.

Giff liked to write what he called "picturesque speech." He kept a little notepad in his pocket and whenever he saw something that seemed beautiful, he'd write it down. Whenever he heard a joke he liked, he'd write that down, too.

He also kept note of all the words he learned. "You know," he told me, "You need to learn new words; just pick out one from the dictionary once a day." So, I learned some of his words. I remember "perseverance" was one of them.

When Bob Gifford was with us, I learned a good mode of thinking. He inspired me to get out of myself, and look at others to see their needs. He was so non-judgmental that I learned to try and understand others rather than judge them. I learned that, "Good psychology is seeking to understand a person. Bad psychology is seeking to judge them."

Giff would walk up to the tough kids sitting on the step outside Doane's and say, "Hello, men!" and ask them about what they had done in school, helping them see the goodness in themselves. He was so successful at motivating others that he was fondly remembered decades later.

For example, I took all the children up to Elmira in 1969. Camille was fifteen, and Joe (he hadn't yet turned eight) kept running off. We were staying at Mrs. Snyder's rooming house, and the policeman, Officer Scaglione, had to bring Joe back several times. The first time he brought Joe back, he asked me, "How is your brother-in-law?" Turned out he was one of the boys who used to sit on that step. He said, "I owe what I am today to your brother-in-law. Without him I might have been a juvenile delinquent." Giff was so good with them, telling them, "I know just how you feel. I was your age once."

Bob Gifford

When I was in the hospital for a week with knee surgery, my sister called me nearly every night and, of course, her husband Bob Gifford was there. "You want to talk to Giff?" she'd ask, "He's got something to tell you." He'd ask how I was doing, and when I said I was in a bit of pain, he replied with, "Well, I was thinking that. I've got some jokes I wrote down.

Would you like to hear some jokes? They might take your mind off the pain."

Jeanette and Bob lived in a white duplex with red shutters in Elmira, and that's why I always wanted a white house with red shutters. An Egyptian couple lived in the other half with their baby. Theirs was an arranged marriage, and they would say, "Love comes with the second child." Jeanette and Bob had their first baby, Brian in 1949, followed by Barbara (Grace) in 1951.

1968 Brian, Jeanette, Barbara (Grace), and Bob

New York City - 1950

I went to New York as soon as I got out of high school. Aunt Mabel took me down there when I was eighteen years old and put me up in the YWCA. She wanted me to go to the Conover Career Girl School which was run by Candy Jones, Harry Conover's wife. Harry owned the high fashion Conover Model Agency, where top models like Candy made $20 an hour.

Janice

New York was such an exciting place, and I was so interested to learn. Manhattan had all these ethnic neighborhoods: Italian, Spanish, Latin American, Chinese, and Indian with restaurants and shops. I started out teaching ballroom dancing at Julie's Dance Studio, but quit and got a job at Zenith Hearing Aid purging files. But, I came down with the three-day measles and had to take the train back to Ithaca, a terrible nine-hour trip, sitting next to a guy who didn't like the idea I had the measles.

While I was home recovering, I spent some time with my four-times-removed-cousin, Charles, on my father's side. Charles was twenty years older than I, an award-winning photographer and recovering alcoholic, who only drank coca cola with a little fresh lemon floating on the top. Charles lived with his mother and her two sisters in a three-story house with their German shepherds. When they had company, they put those dogs in the kitchen and didn't let them out.

Charles told me about two of his best friends, Cappy Gardner, and her husband, Graham. She was a model at The Ford Modeling Agency, and Graham was the director of Bates Fabrics. He suggested I get in touch with them, and when I did, they said, "Come on out!" So he and I did a couple of photo shoots and sent them to Cappy. The sheets of pictures he took included some of me in my bathing suit, the classic pose where you lie down on the floor with your face in your hands looking up. We knew that if the bathing suit pictures somehow got published, I wouldn't be able to work in high fashion, but these were for Cappy.

The pictures went over well, and I went to live with Graham and Cappy Gardener in their Forest Hills penthouse in Queens. Every night they'd come home and have dinner at eight. (Which reminds me of the Frank Sinatra song):

She likes the free fresh wind in her hair,
Life without care
She's broke and it's okay
Hates California, its cold and it's damp
That's why the lady is a tramp

She gets too hungry to wait for dinner at eight
She loves the theatre but never comes late
She'd never bother with people she'd hate
That's why the lady is a tramp

Cappy Gardner took me into The Ford Modeling Agency once, and the way they talked in there! Eileen Ford was her own secretary and everything. She'd have two phones, one on each shoulder, talking with two different people at once. I recently read that The Ford Modeling Agency is the biggest agency going now. (In 2016, Ford Models were making anywhere from $88,000 a year to $355 an hour.)

Cappy and Graham would invite friends over, serve hors d'oeuvres and drinks, and stick something in the oven for dinner. She liked avocados. It was the first time I'd ever tasted an avocado, and I thought they were so good! One evening, her best friend, Peter Bash, a high fashion model photographer, was over and said Kathleen Barnett, the director of Vogue magazine, was looking for a fresh face. She wanted someone from the country, for the April issue. "This girl has it!" he said about me. "I'll do a composite of her."

So, we had a date for a photo shoot in Central Park and other places in New York. It was safe in the morning, whereas it wasn't in the evening. They had to chain the trees at night!

That was when they first came out with the Rolleiflex, a small camera you could click, click, click, click and take a lot of on-the-spot pictures. There was a woman who had a house on 8th Avenue and made the clothes for the models, and she lent me some outfits to wear during the photo shoot. Unfortunately, these clothes had no shape at all.

After Cappy looked at the composite pictures, Peter's proof sheets, she said, "Your figure is just perfect, but I only have one complaint; you've got a big derriere, and you've got to get that down. You face is really pretty." She liked everything else, especially my tiny waist.

Janice

The young model

So! She signed me up, and I was gonna do this! Lo and behold, I got mononucleosis just before this big shoot. "This is no good!" Graham said, and he took me to the drugstore for medicine. But it didn't help. I was cold, then sweating, and I just wanted to sleep all the time. They took me to the doctor. I was so bad off; I had to go on back home to Ithaca.

I slept four hours on my first day home, and woke up with a beet red face and a temperature of 104. My mother came home from the Sugar Bowl, saw me, and called our family doctor, Dr. Frost. He ordered an ambulance right away and had a real worried look. We all went up together, my mother and the doctor. You know I had it so bad I was in the hospital for a whole month?! And then I was home for two months before I was able to return to work.

So, the time for the photo shoot came and went, and I didn't get to be the fresh spring face in the April 1951 edition of Vogue. God had different plans for me.

After I got well, I went back to working at the Sugar Bowl where I met a man who told me about The Webster Apartments on 34th Street in Manhattan. His girlfriend had lived there, and he thought it would be a good fit for me, plus my mother was getting worried about me just hanging around the store.

The Webster was charity housing that charged rent on a sliding scale according to income, built by a man named Webster for out-of-town girls. Girls from the country could live at The Webster for seven years (they later changed that to three years), giving them a chance to find a railroad apartment. Railroad apartments were four apartments to a building; cold-water flats where you had to heat up your water.

So, I returned to New York, and my friend Gail Boker and I lived in the Webster Apartments on 34th Street between 8th and 9th Avenues. We each had a bedroom. You could sign up to use a kitchen or a beau room to entertain guests, but they'd come by every fifteen minutes to check. We ran out in our bathrobes to the newsstand on 8th Avenue because Gail always liked to read *The New York Times* when it came out at night.

I lived on the twelfth floor at 1206. Gail and I liked to visit a girl on the third floor, and I was surprised that she had her windows open without any screens, since her apartment was so much closer to the ground than ours up there on the twelfth floor. "Oh aren't you afraid you'll get bugs? I asked, and she said "No, because bugs don't fly that high." She never had anything like ants or cockroaches. It was a very clean place to live.

And, I enrolled in the Conover Career Girl School run by Candy Jones. Candy was a top model making $20 an hour, compared to my friend, Cappy Gardener, who was only making $7.50 an hour as a model.

One day, I was summoned to Candy Jones' office. "Sit down," she said "How do you like it here? You are doing very well. How would you like to see South Pacific? I can get you a seat in the sixth row." I said that I didn't know what South Pacific was, but I had heard of it. "Well," she said, "It is the show on Broadway right now. Here are the tickets, and you can take a friend."

I worked as a sales girl for Arnold Constable, about a block up from Lord and Taylor and right across the street from the 42nd Street library. My friends from Arnold Constables and I would take our lunch to eat on the benches on the library grounds.

I modeled clothes for people who came in to shop. They made me feel important, too, because the customers liked my advice. For example, they came out with a fur coat that was cut like a sports coat. "This is the latest thing," they said, "What do you think?" "Well, I wouldn't buy it!" I'd tell them, "If I'm going to buy a fur coat, I want it to look like a fur coat" I made $37.50 a week, almost $20 more a week than I would have made working as a sales girl in Ithaca.

Later, they put me in the art department as a model with another girl. She had one of the two artists, an older lady. I had the other, a nice looking twenty-six-year-old English girl from London. I didn't have to get in until after ten in the morning, but I made the same money. The artists painted pictures that went into *The New York Times* every evening.

These girls would try to make their ink washes look like Lord and Taylor's. Lord and Taylor was the "bee's knees" as they used to say; the "cat's meow." I'd have to stand there for so long that my feet felt like they were growing down into the floor. It was so boring! They really liked what I did, so they wanted me for all their fashion shows because they could get me cheaper.

The Nice Guy in the Subway

When I returned to New York, I was still very new to the city. I wanted to meet my girlfriend at Columbia at the Lion's Den but I got on the wrong train and ended up in Harlem. The Lion's Den was on campus, had a soda fountain, and was a good place to meet people. My friend was going to be there when she got out of class and had invited me to meet her there, so I could get to know some people my age.

There were three trains, and I got on one of the trains to Harlem by mistake. It was a lovely spring day, and I was all dressed up with makeup coming from career school. I came up out of the subway, looked around, and saw that I was the only white person there! I knew I was in the wrong place, but I didn't really want to go back down into the subway because it seemed scary down there.

A bus came along, and the driver was a white man, old enough to be my grandfather. He stopped in the middle of the road, opened the bus door, and said, "Lady, you're lost! Where are you headed?" I told him Columbia University, and he said, "I can't take you there but where did you come from?" So I told him 34th Street and he said, "Come onto the bus and I can get you close to there."

The next morning, I saw my friend at career school, and she said, "Gee, where were you, what happened?" I told her I got off at the wrong stop and ended up in Harlem, and she said "Don't give up. Before you get on, just look around to see if anyone has books in their hand and they'll be going to Columbia."

The next day, I tried again. I went down to the subway and looked for someone with books. I saw a nice clean-cut guy, dressed in a suit and carrying books. So, I went over to him and asked if he was going to Columbia University, and he said "Yes." I told him what had happened the day before and how I wanted to make sure and get off in the right place. He said, "Yes, just stay on as long as I stay on."

So we rode together and I learned his name was John. We both got off the subway, and I thought he would just tell me how to get to the Lion's Den and go on his way, but he said, "Oh, I'll just walk you over." And once we got to the Lion's Den, I thought John would go to class or the library or wherever he was headed to. But, when we reached the Lion's Den, he came right in with me. I was so surprised. My girlfriend saw us come in together, and she looked surprised, too. The next day, she told me she was thinking, "Boy, you work fast!"

We stayed there for close to an hour, and John stayed too, entering into the conversation as much as he could. When we left, he accompanied me home. He told me he worked at the Shubert Theater and invited me to see "Paint Your Wagon," saying he could get me a front row seat. "But it doesn't start until 8 o'clock, so would you go out to dinner with me before the show?" I said "Yes," and so he took me to the Plaza, one of the most expensive places in town. Dinner cost $25 for each one of us! That was a lot of money back then when you could get a hamburger at White Tower for ten cents.

After dinner, John got me settled in my seat and went backstage to work. He met me after the show, and he took me home in a cab. We took cabs a lot after that. It was the quickest way to get around in New York. We continued dating and went together for over a year before we got married.

John and Janice - a fashionable pair

John took me to many different restaurants and for buggy rides in Central Park. He always dressed well and said he'd like to have a silver-tipped walking stick someday. Like the one in the movie "Showboat. It got to be a ritual where I'd meet him at the theater between the shows. I would sit at the stage door and wait for John, so I got to see the actors coming and going. One night Rex Harrison, who was starring with his wife Lily Palmer in "Sleeping Beauty," paid me a compliment, saying, "Who is this pretty girl?" on his way past me.

Dancing

John used to take me out dancing. There was this Palladium Ballroom that Marlon Brando liked to go to. A big ballroom like in the movies. There was another ballroom, too, that wasn't just Latin music. It was like the one in the movie where Fred Astaire and Debbie Reynolds played brother and sister. John took me to both of them to dance with professional dancers in the theater. So, I would dance the cha cha with a professional dancer. I remember saying "This must be boring as all get-out to you," because he would sometimes dance with one of the other professional dancers. I wasn't a dancer, but I loved to dance. They were such nice people, and some of them were probably cast in Broadway hits like "Paint Your Wagon" or "Can-Can," the play John took me to soon after we met. They couldn't drink or smoke because they had to keep themselves healthy to dance.

I was interested in ballet and John said he knew a good place to go to learn ballet, so I started going to Ballet Arts in the Carnegie Hall building.

John would take me out to eat at a Mexican or Latin restaurant after the show, and we would see Latin orchestra leaders Tito Puente or Tito Rodrigues both of whom ate there, too. They spoke English, but were from South America. I went to Casa Manao to get recordings of their music. They had just come out with long playing records, or LPs.

JOHN

Camille: I learned a little about my father's childhood from his mother, Nana, who always referred to him as Johnny, just as she referred to my brother as Johnny. Based on the context of our conversation, I could usually tell whether she was talking about my father or my brother.

Helen and John at the beach

My father's brother, Frank, was six years older, nearly the same age difference as between my mother and her older sister. Nana gave birth to Frank when she was seventeen, and he weighed twelve pounds. She was traveling with the show at the time, and baby Frankie slept in a dresser drawer.

Mother and son both developed lice from these lodging conditions.

At first I thought my father must have been a lonely child like my mother had been, but Nana did not have to work outside the home. Also, when my father was six, there were five kids in the house after his parents took in the three Wallace kids (see The Orphans.)

Nana told me that my father liked to play with explosives as a boy. She said the fire department roared up their dirt road on several occasions to douse the woods after things had gotten out of hand. He facilitated similar projects as an adult. I remember my brothers eagerly focused on the pile of gun powder in the bird bath behind the house in West Long Branch.

John, his father, Frank, and his brother, Frank

My father loved photography and had a nice black and white darkroom set up in her basement. I'm sure he was influenced by Stevie Wallace, one of the "orphans." Stevie became a professional photographer and likely helped my father set up his darkroom.

My father was super smart and loved to read. Nana told me he started reading her the Sunday funnies when he was only three years old. She said he read the dictionary page by page. His teachers loved him, and one remarked she could tell when he was coming without looking, because he smelled like soap.

Cartographer Sargent John Illo 1945

My father's older brother, Frank, was keen to join the troops fighting World War II, and at sixteen, had already reached six foot one. At that time, Nana enrolled him in Admiral Farragut Academy, a newly-founded college prep/military style school for Boys in nearby Toms River. After finishing high school, Frank worked for marine engineers. When he was twenty-two, he enlisted in the Marine Engineering Division, and participated in the assaults on Guam and Saipan. Although he was not accordingly ranked, he twice led a battalion into battle. My father was drafted into the regular Army, but with his brains, they gave him a job making maps.

When I was young, my father and his brother drank beer from frosted mugs their mother kept in a mini fridge on the back porch outside the kitchen. We kids knew not to pour milk into those beer mugs.

My father read "The New York Times", drew cartoons, cracked jokes, and took beautiful photographs. He'd find exotic recipes in the Times and make the kitchen smell like faraway places. I loved his Chicken Tandoori and looked forward to Sunday morning pancakes he made into animal shapes on a huge electric griddle.

John and Frank

Janice: John was born April 10, 1926 at the Bronx Maternity Hospital, in New York City, and lived with his parents and older brother, Frank in Manhattan. They named him Johnny in reference to the stage couple, "Frankie and Johnny."

John's cousin Tommy was eleven years younger than he was. Tommy was one of Nana's nephews. His mother Sophie was Nana's younger sister. John wasn't as close to Tom's brother Jimmy, but he and Tommy really took to each other. Tommy called him his teacher.

John and Tommy would talk about what Nana was making for dinner. If John said "I want stew," Tommy would go marching around the dining room table with his stomach out saying, "Vomit, too! Vomit, too!" and Nana would get so mad!

In the fall of 1943, John lived in California and attended UCLA while his dad worked at Treasure Island in San Francisco Bay. They returned in the spring of 1944.

John never learned to swim, something I didn't discover until after we'd been married for over sixty years! He'd go into the ocean but never too far. He was so regular in his sleep habits he never used an alarm clock. It was his habit to watch the sun rise. He once told Camille that if you watch carefully, you can see the rotation of the earth during sun rise.

John Illo, self-portrait

MAKING A FAMILY

Pregnant with Johnny

Bergenfield, New Jersey 1953-1955

We got married in 1953, and after returning from our honeymoon, moved to Bergenfield and lived in a garden apartment at Foster Village on Liberty Road across the street from Teaneck, New Jersey. We paid $90 a month in rent. Each building had four apartments, two up and two down. We lived upstairs. I didn't know anybody around, and it was difficult to find people I could hang out with. Everybody I met over there was on a different schedule from us. John worked at night and their husbands worked during the day. Realizing my dilemma, John hooked me up with Shirley Reilly because her husband also worked at night in either the theatre or at NBC.

I was afraid I wouldn't be able to have any babies because my Aunt Mabel couldn't have children. John even took me to the doctor before we got married, saying, "If it will ease your mind." We found out that I was fine, and he was very happy.

I had two, maybe three periods before we got pregnant with Camille. After the third period, I was crying my eyes out and John said, "Honey, that's normal!" But I kept on crying, sad that I wasn't pregnant. I was certain I wouldn't be able to have any children like my Aunt Mabel, who was unable to bring her babies to term. My Aunt Ibby had six children, and I loved being with them and wanted so much to have a big family of my own. John laughed and said, "No one makes babies every time they make love, some people have to wait a year or longer."

Then, I got what I thought was a virus, and I was vomiting and so sick that I went to the doctor. He said, "That's not a virus, you're pregnant!" And I tell you, when I learned that, I could have jumped over houses. I remember my breasts started to swell and hurt, and the pain was a wonderful reminder, "I'm pregnant!" After that, no matter how sick I felt, I just thought how wonderful it was that I was pregnant.

I couldn't eat much of anything, but I would get these cravings, like strawberries and ice cream. Once in a while, I'd get a craving for this lemon cake with butter cream frosting and unsweetened chocolate dribbled over the top that Nana used to make. When John got home from the theater around 11:30, he'd go back out and look for what I was craving. You know he'd go looking all over Bergenfield. We were so excited to be starting our family!

Camille's Birth Day June 4, 1954

June 3rd was a beautiful day. That's why I thought I'd clean the house and catch up the ironing. We didn't have wash-and-wear clothes back then. I was getting out all the summer clothes and was so excited about my dresses. I always got my hair cut then too, just in time for Father's Day before it gets real hot. The weather was beautiful, and I felt so good.

I don't know why I got dry throat. I guess because it runs in the family. My mother had it. So, I started coughing and John said, "Put your head down," but that didn't help, and then he suggested I lay down. Finally, he brought me a glass of water and said, "Put it on the back of your throat for a while and let it soak in." And that's when my water broke. This had happened to my sister Jeanette, too, when she had her babies. Usually, this happens when the baby is full term, but in my case, it wasn't normal because my due date was a month away.

So, I called the doctor and he said to come to Holy Name Hospital right away, because I was going to have the baby now! John drove me over in the dark, and the stars were out, and I was feeling very happy and peaceful. He commented on how calm I was. I wasn't afraid of the pain because I didn't have any.

After I got to the hospital, I could feel more water coming out, and I worried about that. So I asked the nurse about it, and she said, "Oh, that's just the baby. The baby has to urinate from time to time and that's what you're feeling." I was relieved to hear that this was normal.

It would be another thirty-seven hours before Camille was born the next afternoon. I was reading a book called *Earthquakes and Volcanos*, and the doctor laughed. I asked him why he thought it was funny. "Because you're going to have your own earthquake and volcano soon," He replied, "and I wouldn't think you'd want to read about it." One of the nuns came in and remarked, "That's a good girl to be reading something educational instead of something like *True Confessions*."

First born, baby Camille

I spent the night, and they left the window open. It rained that night, but I didn't feel cold, I told them it felt good, and they told me it was because my body was working and keeping me warm.

When the contractions became painful, just several hours before the baby was born, I thought, "Oh geez, maybe I should get baptized early," in case anything happened, and I died. So, a priest came over and talked with the doctor and said everything was going fine. There was no danger to my life, and it'd be best for me to continue instruction and be baptized later. I was studying to be a Catholic because I had promised to convert during our wedding ceremony. John and his mother wanted the children to be raised in the Catholic Church.

So that's what we decided to do, and I prayed to God that I'd survive. Camille was the first, and I didn't have my mother there to tell me what to expect. Camille was a breech baby, just like I was for my mother, and I remember how painful it was for her to have me.

Thankfully, the doctors had found a better way to deliver a breech baby than how they did it when my poor mother had me. What they did was cut me, so there would be enough room for the baby to come out without tearing me, and that's why Camille's head was so perfectly shaped. She came out feet first, and her head didn't get deformed from the push through the birth canal.

I was surprised by her head of black hair and thought she looked like a coconut. I'd expected her to be bald like other babies, and later learned that premature babies are born with hair which would have disappeared before they were born had they remained in the womb for the full nine months.

They kept the baby in a heated crib, but they didn't give her oxygen. We were afraid they were going to keep her longer, and I wanted to take my little coconut home. Her head was just so perfect with all that dark hair.

But they had to make sure she was gaining weight. I tried to nurse, but since Camille was a preemie, she wasn't strong enough to suck. They used a breast pump to extract the first mother's milk (colostrum) containing the all-important immune serum, and gave it to the baby. After three days, they decided it would be better to put her on formula which we put in a bottle. They cut a crisscross in the nipple so she wouldn't have to suck; the milk would just pour out.

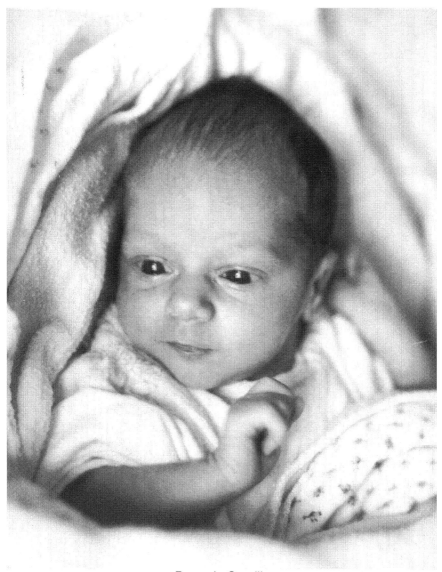

Preemie Camille

Oh, when I had the stitches; that was something! They had given me ether at the time the baby was leaving my body. I was coming out of it when they started to sew me up, and it made me feel like everything kept going over and over again. They only gave me four stitches but it felt like sixteen or twenty, and I yelled each time. There were words that kept getting repeated, too. I couldn't remember what the words were when I came to, only that they made me feel terrible. I couldn't wait for them to be finished.

I didn't realize until later that I was allergic to ether, and that was what was giving me a bad trip. I later learned I was allergic to Demerol and codeine, too.

The first time I had ether was when I had my tonsils out in high school, and it didn't bother me like it did this time. It was like laughing gas. (Chuckling) It was delightful! And every time I laughed, it was this wonderful, relaxed laugh. The nurse would laugh, too saying, "Well, listen to her! She's supposed to go to sleep, not laugh."

When I finally came to, I was not in any pain, and John was sitting beside me. He had waited until after Camille was born to tell my mother about the new baby. Mother sent me flowers; they were snapdragons, and I fell in love with them at that time. They were so delicate and in such great colors.

There were four of us in the hospital, all nursing our babies. There were windows all around, and in the center, was a beautiful statue of Mary. I had learned through my instructions that Mary was our mother, and I felt so happy. I just couldn't wait to get home to John because of my understanding of how Mary had the joy of giving birth to Jesus in the presence of her husband, Saint Joseph.

After having a daughter, we thought we'd have a bunch of girls like Marguerite Lyons, who had five daughters. At home, I was changing our baby and putting her in a new receiving blanket with John looking on, and he said, "Now I know my mommy loved me very much," and I asked him, "What made you say that?"

"Because, I love Camille so much."

Johnny's Birth Day September 7, 1955

It was three weeks past my due date and I was huge! I couldn't seem to get Johnny to budge. One thing I tried was to go out with my friend Shirley to an Alex Guinness movie. I always laughed and laughed at these movies, and I thought that would help.

We thought something would get started, but I was praying my water wouldn't break on the bus. From Foster Village, we could take a bus in to New York across the George Washington Bridge, and then go down into the subway, which would take us to the movie district. So, I had gotten a babysitter to sit with baby Camille, and we went to the movies. I had a great time, sitting there laughing my head off, sure that this would do it, but nothing happened.

I called the doctor, and he suggested I come to Holy Name Hospital so he could break my water. Everything went smooth. Again, they gave me ether, but this time it didn't bother me, and I think Johnny was born a couple of hours later at 4:00 in the afternoon. He was a big boy, over eight pounds, much bigger than Camille, who was so little.

Later, when John and I got our first look at the new baby, we thought he looked like an old man. He had light blond hair; he was a tow head. John nicknamed him "the old philosopher." I remember Sister Consolada saying he was the brightest in her class. John was happy to have a son. It didn't matter to me whether we had a boy or a girl, but John was hoping for a boy because we already had a girl.

When we got home, we were getting ready to move because we had bought our first house in Bergenfield. We brought Johnny home, and he slept in the bassinette in our bedroom. Johnny was only five weeks old when we moved into our new house and still slept with us in our bedroom.

John worked in the city, and Bergenfield was only a fifteen minute drive from the George Washington Bridge. Johnny used to wake up at night when John came home from the theatre at around midnight. He would be so full of life, laughing and laughing. "Oh, he's bright!" John would say.

Janice, Johnny, and Nana

One day, the insurance man came over and I had to sign some papers. I had Johnny in my arms and the man said, "Here, I'll hold the baby," and little Johnny looked up and smiled, which delighted the man. Johnny was happy to be with anyone.

John and I would have our snacks, and we'd bring Johnny down and put him in the playpen. John liked seeing the kids at night, but Camille didn't wake up. Johnny would be jumping up and down in the playpen, laughing and laughing with that smile he had with his tiny little mouth, giggling and laughing.

John would give him little things to eat, whatever we were eating. Given John's history with allergies, the doctor told us to just put little bits of food in front of the baby, and if he wanted more, to give him more. The theory was that if the child was allergic to something, he wouldn't eat it. But Johnny liked it all and ate a little bit of everything until he was eight years old and ran into trouble with orange juice in West Long Branch. Oh, he liked it, but it made his hands and feet swell.

Years later, Michael had this same reaction to orange juice.

The Bergenfield House

In October, 1955, when Johnny was five weeks old, we bought a two-bedroom house in Bergenfield. It was in a residential area on a road that was all dug up with broken cement. When the cab driver brought us there he said, "This road is rock and roll!"

At 8:00 in the morning, the day after we moved in and had been up all night setting up beds and getting settled, we heard a bulldozer knocking over the tree that our clothesline was attached to. On the one side of our new driveway the neighbor had planted a pretty rock garden with flowers. Meanwhile, on the other side, they were tearing up the ground to build a house which was to be completed in only six months.

We had been under the impression from the realtor that our property line included that tree with our clothesline on it. Being first time home buyers, we hadn't thought to look that carefully at the deed. John was so angry, he went right down to *The New York Times* and put in a "for sale" ad for the house.

To make things worse, I had this bladder infection and a fever which was my reaction to the antibiotics. So, I was going up and down the stairs because there wasn't a bathroom downstairs, and also putting up wall paper. We didn't have a washing machine so I was washing sheets and everything by hand in the kitchen sink. And John put up some clotheslines down in the basement.

I got bursitis in my wrist, which became acute four years later. I could feel it all the way up to my elbow. Dr. Stone took one look at me (he had a habit of standing in front of you and taking a good look) and then he walked over and pressed my shoulder, and I hit the ceiling! I told him that when we first moved into our house I had to do the washing by hand. He asked me if I had to wring them out by hand, too and I said, "Oh, yes," and he said, "That would do it!"

We were still in Bergenfield when my mother sent me an automatic washing machine. She didn't use one because she only had her uniform to wash out. She washed it every night and hung it on the curtain rod in the bathroom. Most everybody else was using an automatic washer. Before then, they were all using the wringer type.

So, we got this automatic washing machine and didn't realize you had to bolt them onto the concrete. During the first load, it started going boom, boom, boom, boom, boom, and it was coming right towards me! It looked like it was walking, like a robot, walking right towards me, and fast! I got ahold of myself and grabbed the plug (the thing nearly hit me) and pulled it from the wall. We had to bolt it down before we could use it again.

We celebrated Camille's second birthday in the Bergenfield house as well as Johnny's baptism, when he was nearly a year old, because I had finally got my fever gone. We had put it off because of my poor health and the move. He was nine months old when we had him baptized, and we threw a nice party with about thirty people, mostly family. My mother came down to help me.

Billy and Ann Kominsky, (Nana's brother Al's son and his wife), were there. The four of us liked to go out on Sundays for picnics. They lived in New Milford, a couple of miles away from Bergenfield. There were a lot of Catholics who lived around us on that street, and many of them came. We had the Navas, who lived in Brooklyn. Vinny Nava was John's best friend and they had met at Fordham University. We loved going over there with the kids. They were a big Italian family who happily passed baby Johnny all around while Camille ran everywhere.

My cousin, Beverly Zimmer, came to Johnny's baptismal party and brought him a nursery song book, which had all of these nursery rhymes with the music to them. Johnny wanted me to read that book over and over and sing the rhymes. That was when I started reading to my children.

Johnny looked at that book all the time or had it in his lap. We had a piano, but he didn't play it. John worked as a stage hand for the first three years of our marriage, and because he worked at night, I had to keep Camille and Johnny quiet during the day so he could sleep.

Silver-Tipped Cane

After we'd been married a few years, I went to Abercrombie and Finch and bought John a silver-tipped walking stick for $50. It took me a few years to save up for it. John gave me $20 a week for groceries and such, but I actually only needed $15 a week. "Well, you can put that in the bank," John said, regarding the extra. When I bought the walking stick, Nana was so proud. "I always thought Johnny and Janice had good taste!" she said.

Becoming Catholic

I mistakenly thought that the only difference between Catholic and Protestant was the way people worshiped. I loved my upbringing in the Methodist church and didn't think there was any difference in the biblical teachings. I had no desire to leave the Methodist Church.

But when I went to my first mass with John, before we were married, I heard about the Eucharist and asked him about it when we got home. "I didn't remember learning about this," I told him, and he said, "You didn't. The Catholic Church is the only one that believes that." And I said, "Well, that's just what the bible says: take this and eat, etc." John replied, "Well, maybe Honey would like to take instructions." And I said, "Yes, I'd like to take instruction and learn about the teachings of the Church."

So I went over to the Holy Name Church in Teaneck and started learning more about the teachings of the Catholic Church. It was six weeks of instructions, and they gave me transportation back and forth while John was teaching. Meanwhile, I had a babysitter for Camille. Protestants stop going to church after confirmation, but Catholics continue their education by attending CCD (Confraternity of Christian Doctrine) classes.

I loved the instructions! There were about 100 people from the church itself, many of them Franciscans, to support those of us who were learning. I thought that perhaps I might want to join their order. It was after that I was baptized a Catholic in Saint John's the Evangelist in Bergenfield.

Clare Boothe Luce was a convert who used to say, "You can't leave your mind at the door of the Catholic Church," meaning, you can't just come in on a feeling and say the Holy Spirit is moving you. I liked having to think about my faith.

On City Island, I used to take the kids to Saturday evening confession, and this is when I first learned of the Carmelite order. I hadn't been confirmed yet, and my faith was being shaken by Jehovah's Witnesses and Mormons, who were coming to my door and sharing stories from the bible. I confided in my neighbor Lil, and she asked me if I'd been confirmed. When I said no, she said that I needed to do that and get the power of the Holy Spirit.

After I converted, I began reading about the lives of the saints and my mother said, "If you love reading the saints; you have a saint in the family!" Arthur Horton, her older brother, drowned when he was eighteen, and the whole town went half-mast. Even though he was so young, he belonged to a group that went around and helped people. So everyone in town loved Arthur because he loved helping people, fixing things, and helping repair houses.

After we moved to Shippensburg, I picked up a Carmelite pamphlet from a table out in front of the church. I liked what they said about "finding the mystic within you", and in 1975, I became a Carmelite under their secular arm.

Norvelt, Pennsylvania - 1956-1957

It took us nine months to sell the Bergenfield house and move to Norvelt, Pennsylvania, just outside of Pittsburgh. It was September of 1956, shortly after Johnny's first birthday, and I recall moving in a week or two ahead to get the place set up. Camille and Johnny stayed with Nana while we made the transition. We'd been living out of boxes until then because we thought we might move any day.

Norvelt was named after Eleanor Roosevelt. It was one of dozens of "Subsistence Homesteads" developed by President Roosevelt as part of the New Deal. It had a grocery store, a luncheonette, a doctor, and a dentist. For anything else, we went up to Mt. Pleasant. Each house was built the same, a little frame Cape Cod, the kind I always loved with the dormers and a chicken coop in every yard so that, as FDR had promised, there could be a chicken in every pot.

John had begun his master's work a couple of nights a week at the University of Pittsburgh and had gotten his first teaching job at Saint Vincent College, run by Benedictine monks, in Latrobe, about eleven miles from Norvelt. Even though his pay dropped from $176 to $60 a week, we were very happy. We were on a normal schedule!

Our college friends were married couples, and we'd have each other over to our homes. There were faculty parties, too. We just had a real nice social life that we didn't have when John was working in the theater. In Bergenfield, we lived high off the hog, but it was a topsy turvy world because of John's late night schedule.

Camille called our home in Norvelt the barn house because it was so big, so we called it that, too. Built before the depression, the house sat at the top of the hill along a circular road; a brick mansion, with enormous stone steps. John took a great photo of the four of us sitting on those steps using his tripod. He dabbled in photography and had a darkroom set up in the basement of his mother's house in Atlantic Highlands.

We rented the whole upstairs, seven rooms with a laundry room and everything. John used to take his chair out on the roof over the porch and sit in the sun. The couple who rented the first floor of the mansion had three boys the kids liked to play with. Their mother was pregnant with their fourth child.

John, Janice, Johnny, and Camille on the barn house steps

John and his camera

John and I went out to Mt. Pleasant every week. We got a babysitter, one of the teacher's daughters from Saint Vincent, and we would drive past these coke ovens where people had lived during the depression. They would be burning coke as we drove by. There, we went to a bar with a TV and enjoyed an evening of complete sentences without the kids.

On Sundays we'd take the kids to Mt. Pleasant for ice cream cones and white chocolate, John's favorite. Camille was still a baby, only two years old.

Every day in the afternoon after lunch, I liked to relax with some classical music. I enjoyed Brahms, and she and I would just dance all over the room to that music.

I had studied ballet when I was first dating John, and was teaching Camille pirouettes and leaps. She picked it right up even though she was only two years old. We city folks had come to the country! I did the same thing years later with my granddaughter Charity.

Johnny played in his playpen during the day. When our downstairs neighbors moved, heat no longer came up from downstairs, and it was a lot colder on the floor. We didn't notice because the heating vents were mounted on the wall.

Johnny started wheezing, and we couldn't get ahold of the doctor. When I picked him out of the playpen, I realized how cold it was on the floor. He had gotten bronchitis, which had turned into bronchial asthma. It was horrifying to watch his chest cave in when he took a breath. We wrapped him in blankets to make sure he was warm.

Finally, there was a knock at the door and it was the doctor. The doctor said to keep him wrapped up and take him to the hospital. He told us to open the windows of the car so Johnny could get more oxygen on the way. When we arrived, they put him into an oxygen tent overnight and into the next day where I stayed by his side. Thankfully, he recovered quickly and was soon his jovial self again.

Johnny always loved this toy horse, probably because the wheels jangled. There must have been bells on the wheels. He could ride it around the apartment. The rooms were circular in that you could go from one room to the next to the next and all the way back to the first room. So round and round he'd ride this little horse, pushing himself with his feet.

But one time, he went down the stairs on his horse, and it was a long stairway. We hadn't figured out how to block the stairs off in the house like we did in our Foster Village home.

Thankfully, the door at the bottom was closed because that door went to the stone steps outside the house. He was still sitting on his horse as it bumped on down the stairs. As I remember, he didn't get hurt at all. And then we realized we needed to put a gate at the top of the stairs.

Johnny walked earlier than Camille did, and he would stand up in his crib. He started to talk early, too. One day he looked out the window and said "buh-dy buh-dy!" At first I didn't know what he was saying because he couldn't pronounce his R's yet, but then he pointed. I looked where he pointed and saw the bird flying and realized he was saying birdie. Most children's' first words are mommy or daddy but, "buhdy" was Johnny's first word.

Those were wonderful days that we spent in Norvelt because John would take us on picnics. Every Sunday we'd just drive along until we saw a place we thought would be nice and set up our lunch. Norvelt was a small, rural town in Western Pennsylvania so we never had to drive far to find a magical place. When we lived on City Island, a couple of moves later, we used to dream of living in the country with rolling hills and that's just how it was in Norvelt.

This reminds me of a song:

It's a lazy afternoon
And the beetle bugs are zoomin'
And the tulip trees are bloomin'
And there's not another human in view
But us two...

One balmy day, we came to a place where the ground was all golden, like blonde hair. It was warm and we all felt happy. After we ate, we would walk around and explore. We had all these wonderful discoveries together on Sunday afternoons.

One such day, we decided to start early in the morning and go looking for the Appalachian Mountains. We packed up the kids and a tablecloth that we could spread on the hood of the car for a picnic. Every time we'd reach the top of a foothill and look over it we'd see a valley beyond and decide to go on to the next. We spent six hours that day searching for the Appalachians. Camille and Johnny had a great time in the back seat of the car and were never bored.

We took four trips to Nana's that year, which was a long way in the car. John was so good at keeping the kids entertained, they never raised a fuss. Both of us cried when we left Norvelt because we were so happy there. And John never cried. That was the year he took us to the opera to see

"Camille." The tears were coming down his face, not only from the sadness of the story, but because he was going back to the theater. I mean, tears just came down. We'd spent all of our savings, trying to live on his teacher's salary. We just couldn't live on $60 a week.

Fair Haven, New Jersey - 1957-1958

So we moved to Fair Haven because it was close to John's mother (Nana) and much closer to New York than the six-to-eight hour commute from Norvelt. Even so, it took him two hours to drive into the city. He'd go into work in the afternoon for three or four hours, and then he'd drive the two hours home. He wouldn't even get back until 2:00 a.m. I'd wait up, and we'd have something to eat.

Neither the New York Turnpike nor the Garden State Parkway had been built back then. John would say "Look at the guerrilla snot!" when we reached what they called Vanderbilt's Folly, an unfinished tunnel through the Blue Ridge Mountains on the Pennsylvania Turnpike. And it's true; the shelves of frozen water dripping from the rock cliffs did resemble snot. After they finished construction, he could make that drive in only an hour.

Things were rough until he got the job at Monmouth College. And then life was so much better. We have wonderful memories of Fair Haven after John left the theater. Camille and Johnny would come to our downstairs bedroom early in the morning, and we'd wake to see them on either side of our bed.

Irene's husband Nicky would always come around just before lunch and give the kids some money and tell them to go buy some ice cream. He was getting John back for doing this with his daughters Linda and Barbara when they were growing up. John would come around in his Model A before lunch and give Nicky's girls money to buy ice cream and ruin their lunch.

Camille's fourth birthday in Fair Haven

We were in Fair Haven when Camille turned four, and John climbed a tree to take pictures of her birthday party. He was a talented photographer with a number of cameras and took stunning portraits and landscapes. He passed his talent down to our kids, notably Johnny.

City Island, Bronx, New York 1958 - 1962

In 1958, John went back to working at the theater, and the four of us moved from Fair Haven to a little bungalow on City Island. Ann Somnitz was a wardrobe mistress at the main Shubert Theater when John's father, Frank Illo, was head carpenter for all eleven Shubert Theaters. Ann had a big house on the far end of City Island, near a park with a gazebo that was used for one of Elizabeth Taylor's movies. When Ann found out John was looking to move up to New York she told him about a house for rent on City Island Avenue.

So we rented the house. It had a nice back yard, half of which we decided to keep free from mowing so the kids would have exposure to the natural world. Roses, blackberries, raspberries, and praying mantises grew in a tangle on the wild side.

When Camille was little, she liked to pick up snakes even though my mother said, "Don't ever pick up the snakes because you might be picking up a bad one." One day when we were living on City Island she brought a snake into the house. And I said, "No, no, no!" and then it was in the house, and we couldn't find it.

She kept saying, "Where 'nake?! Where 'nake?!" She was only four and couldn't pronounce her "S's." It was no bigger than a large worm! Camille also had a set of little plastic animals she took everywhere we went in a little satchel.

There was a little sidewalk that went half way across the yard and a terrace where the kids used to play with an old water heater. Our kids and their friends would balance atop the heavy steel cylinder in their bare feet and roll it back and forth across the terrace. If they used one foot with more force than the other, it would veer off course towards the house or down the slope into the rest of the yard. Then they would have to roll it back into place, perpendicular to the house.

Those two rooms upstairs were really an attic with a raised roof. Camille, Johnny, and Bobby slept in one of the upstairs rooms. John used the other room as his office, but then we decided it was too much to have three children in one room, so we split the kids between two rooms and he set up his office in the porch room downstairs. It was pretty, with its own door and little walkway that went around. And then summer came, and we wanted to get the kids out of that hot room and into the porch room, so we moved them downstairs and John got the hot room upstairs.

Johnny and Janice in the City Island Kitchen

Our neighbors, Lilian Brown (Lil) and her husband, had one son, Rossie, and they adopted Louie. Louie had been a foundling child meaning he had been abandoned and institutionalized. They wanted to adopt someone that they could really help. They let Rossie pick him out, and he picked four-year-old Louie. When they first saw him he was in a playpen on his back, arms flying around everywhere, and he had a bottle. They said that's all he could do; he couldn't eat or drink because he had cerebral palsy.

They changed Louie's life just by loving him. Lil would sit in a chair and put Louie on her lap, with his little arms flying and hold him down on her lap until, little by little he got relaxed and settled down. She was determined not to put him down until he made some progress. By the time we met Louie, he was about eleven or twelve, eating and drinking, walking and talking like normal children. Lil was taking him down to the corner and waiting with him to take the bus to a Catholic School for retarded people. He did well with it.

Three-year-old Johnny liked Louie as a friend. The Browns invited Johnny to sleep overnight in their back yard. Louie could barely see. He had to hold things right up to his eyes to see them, but he could see the moon, which was out that night. "What's that white thing up there?" he asked Johnny.

As Louie progressed he started to act more his age, and he began to outgrow Johnny. "What's wrong with Louie?" Johnny asked, "He's not as friendly as he used to be." I tried to explain Louie's condition; that he was really much older, but I don't know if Johnny understood.

Years later Mr. Brown had a fatal heart attack while driving in Maine with Louie in the car. Louie was able to turn the car off to prevent a crash.

~*~

There was a lot of fungus on City Island because it was damp. One side was more sheltered than the other, probably a good breeding ground for fungus. There were houseboats on the sheltered side with flowers in window boxes. The people who lived in the houseboats were ne'er do wells, and liked to drink. Lil was everybody's friend, so one woman came asking for money, but Lil refused, offering anything in her refrigerator instead.

When we went to the doctor, Dr. Stone, he shone a black light on our skin and noted that everything that turned pink was a fungus. His office was in Fordham, forty-five minutes away. We had to go on the bus. Bobby, our third child, would pack his crayons and coloring books. Johnny loved to go to the pharmacy down the hall. I assumed he went to talk with the pharmacist. So I went down to see if he was bothering the pharmacist and he said, "Oh you're the mother of Greased Lightning!"

I recently asked Johnny, "What was so interesting about that pharmacist?" and Johnny said, "He used to let me ride the dumb waiter."

Years later I took James, our youngest, and his wife Kathryn, over to the public library in Shippensburg. James was telling a story to the nice woman who worked there about how he and his two older brothers, Joe and Michael, liked to climb on the dumb waiter. You can get on it, and it will take you down to the basement or whatever.

Johnny and his wife Darla have a dumb waiter, basically a laundry chute, in their house on Red Oak Lane in Shippensburg, and their grandkids play with it when they visit.

For birthdays, I allowed the kids to have any breakfast cereal they wanted. They would usually choose Cap'n Crunch and Lucky Charms. The rest of the year it was cheerios, shredded wheat, fortified oat flakes, and raisin bran flakes. The only thing I'd let the kids eat before breakfast was animal crackers. And when we went grocery shopping they were allowed to put a penny in the slot at the store and get a sour ball.

We wanted my mother to come live with us after she sold the Sugar Bowl. Mother had already refused to live with my sister Jeanette, her husband Bob, and their two children Brian and Barbara. The only way she would consider living with Jeanette's family is if they gave her a place in the basement so that she could come and go without disturbing the family. Jeanette wouldn't hear of that, and my mother decided against retiring. She felt she would get too bored. Seeing so many people in the hospital who needed care, she took some training and became a nurses' aide.

While we were on City Island, Nana discovered Thrift Shops. She liked a shop called "The Attic" in Fair Haven and would send over clothes for the kids. I never got over the time she bought a delicate, light pink sweater with puffy sleeves and pearl buttons for me. John liked it. He always asked me, "Why do you wear blue and green?"

We went to visit Nana every weekend. One time I asked Nana in the kitchen, "Would you mind if I called you mother?" and she said, "Yes of course!" and we hugged. I don't recall hugging each other like this before. I'd been calling her Helen up to that point which was at least less formal than Mrs. Illo.

Right after we got married, I'd written to her thanking her for all her help with the wedding and used the words "you and Mr. Illo" Nana remarked, "How formal can we get?" so I started calling her Helen. Now I began calling her "Mother."

Eventually John got a job at Iona College in Westchester County and worked at the theater in the evenings and on the weekends. When Camille and Johnny were old enough, they attended Saint Mary Star of the Sea Catholic School, half a mile away, on the bridge end of the island.

Bobby's Birth Day September 16, 1958

I woke up in the morning with labor pains. John was getting ready to go to work. He had just started work as a teacher at Iona College, a Catholic school in New Rochelle, in Westchester County, New York. His first day of his new job just happened to be the same day Bobby decided to come into the world.

John said he was going to stay home and get me to the hospital and I said, "Oh, don't do that! You'll lose your job!" He laughed and said, "This is a Catholic college. They're not going to fire me for taking my wife to the hospital to have our baby!" So I thought that was pretty nice!

I had my bag packed anyway. People do that when they know they're going have a baby soon. I can't remember exactly what his due date was, but it was right around that time.

Bobby wasn't a surprise like Camille being born a month early, or Johnny being born three weeks late.

I think the hospital was Fordham Hospital. We were living in a rental house at 393 City Island Avenue, on City Island in the Bronx. We had saved $1,000 in the bank and had a new car, a 1954 Ford Sedan. John drove me to the hospital when the contractions were twenty minutes apart so we had plenty of time.

Everything was fine. I got in there and it didn't seem to take that long. It wasn't a real hard labor, but they gave me an anesthetic anyway, and Bobby was born before noon.

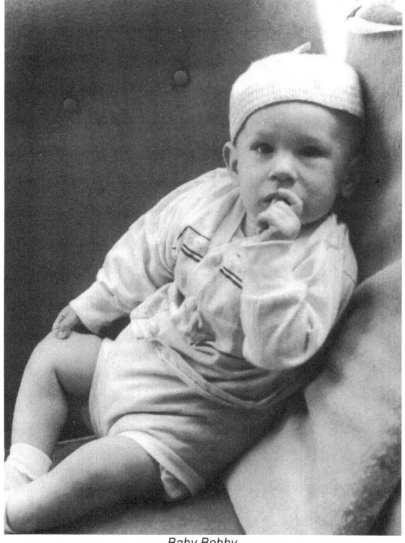

Baby Bobby

I remember hearing a girl crying out and yelling down the hall, when I was back in the recovery room after having Bobby. "Well gee; she already had the baby, why is she yelling now?" I asked. The nurse said, "She had a C-section." This was the only time I encountered a woman who had had a Caesarean section. Most women had their babies naturally back then. The poor woman was still having contractions.

I had gotten the mail that day but didn't open it until after Bobby was born. My mother always sent me pictures of my friends, and she had sent two or three of them. I thought that was a nice thing to open up after having my baby. One of my roommates, an Italian Catholic girl, had her mother visiting and she said, "That must be from your Mama."

I had a great time talking to the girl in the bed on my other side. Her husband was a policeman. He came in and said, "I'm a father now, and if these people want to cut themselves up with knives, I'm just going to stay out of their way!"

When I first saw Bobby, I thought he was beautiful, and that he looked just like Johnny. The other mothers and I always recognized our own babies through the window.

Bobby was the first baby I was able to nurse successfully. Camille received the first mother's milk, but I didn't even try with Johnny. I was healthier after Bobby was born than at any other time. I wasn't worn out like I was after the other children were born. I really felt healthy, and it was sooo good. I felt healthy when I was pregnant with Joe, too. Maybe it had something to do with living so close to the ocean.

Back then we stayed seven days in the hospital. It seemed very short compared to my mother, who stayed thirteen days. One of our friends, a retired nurse said, "It's inhumane, giving them no more rest than seven days." The hospital bill was only $100 with insurance.

Joe's Birth Day December 4, 1961

December 4, 1961 was a very nice day, one of those forty-to-fifty degree winter days. We were living on City Island in the Bronx, and I had a burst of energy early in the day. I had gotten all my cooking done (a stew) and had taken in all the blankets that I'd hung on the line the day before. John always told me to clean them by hanging them on the line, letting the wind, rain, and sun clean them. And it had rained and they had dried in the sun.

So I took a nap, and when I woke up in the early afternoon, before Camille and Johnny came home from school, I started having contractions. Bobby was three years old, so he was already at home with me.

We had some friends who had offered to stay with the kids while I went to the hospital. They lived just this side of the City Island Bridge in a huge house. They took in elderly men as boarders and took care of them, which earned them supplemental income from the government. I called them, but they weren't home so I called Lil, and she wasn't home either.

John was at work, and I didn't know what to do because now my contractions were coming every two and a half minutes. So, I started praying and since by now Camille and Johnny were home from school, I asked them to pray, too.

Johnny had brought a friend home from school for the first time. I had always said, "Anytime you want to bring a friend home, just bring them." I thought it was great that he had brought a friend home but I had to say, "Oh no, this is the wrong day to have your friend over!" Which disappointed Johnny, but we sent his friend home anyway.

Then I saw Lil drive by in her little white car, and I called her on the phone and she said, "Alright, everything will work out." And she came over to drive me to the hospital. The hospital was in the Bronx, so it didn't take long to get over there. The three kids were in the back seat, and Lil asked them if they had a preference for a brother or a sister. We were surprised when all three, even Camille, said they wanted another brother. Lil laughed saying, "If this keeps up, you'll have your own in-built basketball team!"

Janice and baby Joe

We reached a park near the hospital, and I was having a really long contraction that wouldn't end. I was thinking, "Oh boy, I'm going to have this baby now!" And I saw this tree. It was beautiful in the late afternoon sun and seemed to be calling out to me. "Stop right here!" I said to Lilian, "And I'll have my baby under that tree." I was thinking like an animal!

Lil said, "Now, just hold on, we're almost there." But I begged, "Please, please!" because I didn't want to have the baby in the car. She continued driving, and I kept looking wistfully out the window at that tree, thinking, "There goes my chance."

Well, you know when Joe was installed as a pastor and everyone went to the reception they asked me to speak. I talked about how he always loved life. "Joe loved life so much he didn't want to stay in the womb, he wanted to get out and live life," I told them.

Sure enough though, the contraction did end, and I was able to walk up the stairs into the hospital with Lil. I looked on the clock on the wall as we entered, and I remember looking at the time right after Joe was born and realizing he was born only nineteen minutes after I walked into the hospital.

When we first arrived, they sent me over to this one person who was working at the desk. She was telling me we have to have your name and all this and was asking me all these questions and I said, "I can't wait!" I finally got through to her, and a light bulb went off. "Oh, we got to get her in there!" is what she was thinking. So they sent me straight to the birthing room and gave me Sodium Pentothal. I never even went into the labor room. I'm so glad I didn't have the baby under the tree!

Later they took me down in a wheel chair to the room where all the babies were kept, and when I looked in the window I spotted him right away. "Oh! That's mine!" I said. I knew because he looked just like Johnny and Bobby. Especially Bobby."

When I returned to the room, I was talking to my roommate about how uncanny it is that we can always spot our own baby through the nursery window, and Lil called on the phone. "How does he look to you?" she asked. "He's a little mite with a soul," I told her, and she was delighted with my answer.

I'd brought a book with me, "The Confessions of Saint Augustine." At that time it was required in many universities to read this book and John had given me a copy in Old English. The doctor came into my room, saw it, and said, "That takes me back to my college days!"

After I returned home with the baby, Ann Somnitz came to visit. She was Bobby's Godmother and had lent me a baby carriage for Joe. When she saw him, she couldn't believe it wasn't Bobby. I said "No, that's Jody!"

When Joe was nursing he was so fat, just like Bobby was when I was nursing him. I wondered how they could get fat from what looked like bluish water to me. If I took my breast out, the milk would shoot across the room. I soon reached the point where I couldn't nurse anymore because of a breast abscess. I had a temperature of 104 or 105. Our friend Ellen Goulden took care of baby Joe for a few days, and she and her husband fell in love with him. The doctor said I would never be able to nurse again.

In the old days, when they had no other way of birth control, they would nurse the babies as long as possible. Two years was about it, long enough to prevent pregnancy and give the women a couple of years between babies. But things were changing. What was especially bad was that technology took over. At the time Joe was born, they had just come out with these bottle holders. My friend, Shirley Reilly, used the bottle holder without giving it a second thought, because it made her life easier. I couldn't begin to think about that being alright, and so I never bought anything like that. I was one of a very few that nursed, when I was nursing Bobby and Joe.

Television

Around the time we got our first television On City Island, they took a poll to see how much time people spent watching television, and the average was three hours a day. So

John said, "No more than three hours a week for us." In England, thousands got their minds wrecked from the special effects on TV. They called it TV epilepsy. John made sure we stayed away from the set because the waves came out the sides of the cathode ray tube behind the screen. He also told us not to look at the advertisements. Sometimes he'd get up, turn down the sound, and block our view by standing in front of the set when the ads came on.

It was some fun, TV; movies were such a treat, and here we had all this in our own house! I always liked The Waltons, Little House on the Prairie, Emergency, and Project UFO. I liked some of the Christmas shows like Little Drummer Boy. I didn't like Peanuts because there were no parents. It was just kids living like adults. I liked to watch National Geographic, Wild Kingdom, and Daktari. I liked the early Tarzan movies, but not the later ones with the bad guys. I loved Superman, but not Batman so much.

We would only allow the kids to watch three shows a week, which they would pick out of the TV Guide. I was so proud of them because they never chose anything bad. Same way with the movies. I'd save up money, and once a year we'd go to a movie. I allowed the kids to pick, and they always picked good ones. In 1961, my mother took us to see 101 Dalmatians at the movies, at the matinee.

John's brother Frank worked for NBC, and John worked in the theater as a member of the stagehand father-son union. Frank used to say, "NBC means No Bonus for Christmas." His sons, Frank Sr.'s grandsons, Frank and Mark, work on Broadway, too.

Camille: The New York stagehands' union is officially known as Local One of the Theatrical Protective Union. Local One is a member of the International Alliance of Theatrical Stage Employees and Moving Picture Operators of the United States and Canada. You got into the union if you knew someone, or if your father was in the business.

Jackie Gleason would have these girls who weren't traditional beauties, but there was something different about their chiseled features. We loved watching The Honeymooners with Trixie and Ed Norton, and Abbott and Costello. We especially loved their "Who's on First" routine! I did not like Laurel and Hardy so much growing up or the Three Stooges. I always liked Robert Benchley. When you went to the movie theatre, they showed a short film before the main feature. One of Benchley's pre-movie skits was "How to Sleep." He was very funny, but cool funny, intellectually funny, like British humor.

Johnny, Bobby, and Camille pretending to be a dog

Camille: I remember watching Mr. Wizard with my brothers, waiting for the prop guy to hand the wizard a flask or something. If we saw the hand on TV, we'd jump up and down yelling, "That's daddy's hand!" I was so taken by Lassie that I ran around on all fours making dog noises for at least a year.

Avon-by-the-Sea, New Jersey 1963-1964

We moved from City Island to another rental house in Avon on Bobby's fifth birthday, September 16, 1963. After settling in, the kids were making up songs about their old home, and Bobby wrote a little song that went:

I'm lying on my bed and tears
are falling down into my ears
because I miss the sound
of the fire engines...
Isn't it a pity we had to leave the city!"

We wanted to buy a house in Farmingdale, about fifteen miles from Monmouth College; seventeen acres with two houses, the main house and a smaller one they were renting out. After the van was loaded, and the children packed into our 1954 Ford sedan, John learned the deal had fallen through, leaving us stranded. There was a man there that said to John, "You are a man with a problem." He said he had some storage places (they were chicken coops) we could put our furniture in until we could find another place.

We went to Nana's where John took a moment to devise a solution. He began calling owners of vacation homes on the Jersey shore until he found a furnished rental house on Woodland Avenue in Avon-by-the-Sea that could be rented for the off-season. The house was just a couple of blocks from the ocean, within walking distance of the elementary school, and only a ten-minute car ride from Asbury Park. Camille, Johnny and Bobby went to school there. Joe was one and a half, and I was pregnant with Michael. It was a happy year there, with John teaching classes a couple of nights a week at Monmouth College.

John Fitzgerald Kennedy's Assassination

Camille: I was nine the day JFK died. My brother Michael would make his entrance five days later. It was a pivotal year in many ways. My parents had moved me and my three brothers from City Island in the Bronx to New Jersey, but something went wrong, and they weren't able to move us into our new home. So they rented a nice big house within smelling distance of the Atlantic and kept looking. Avon-by-the-Sea was a resort town, buzzing with vacationers in the summer, and reduced to its core population during the school year. We had a new house, new school, new town, and new friends.

Everyone idolized President Kennedy for his good looks, charming accent, and perfect wife and kids. When our teachers asked us who we most admired, it was him, the youngest president ever and perhaps the most powerful person alive. If the world needed saving, he alone was the man for the job. Our future was safe in his capable hands.

We kids spent our year in Avon growing our moxie muscles, running at large in the quiet streets, and squirming through boarded up windows in the massive hotels on Ocean Avenue. We took turns jumping off the boardwalk, seven feet above the deep beach sand. Or we'd huddle beneath the drawbridge and watch the counterbalance, a piece of concrete the size of a car, grind its way down the wall. After dinner we played "Who Dies the Best" on our sloping front lawn, perfect for rolling down.

None of this prepared us for our fearless leader's death.

Friday, November 22, 1963 started out like any other day. The elementary school was only a few blocks away, so Johnny and I walked. Bobby would have been in kindergarten, so he probably tagged along. I pledged allegiance to the flag in my fourth-grade home room, fidgeting, distracted by the prospect of another delicious weekend.

After lunch, we were unexpectedly herded into the auditorium. My giddiness at the interruption was immediately dampened by the bleak look on my teacher's face. When all the classes had filed in, the principle cleared his throat and said, "The president has been shot. School is dismissed. Go home to your families." No one moved for a minute. The only sound was that of a muffled newscaster on a television backstage.

A classmate asked me to walk her home because she didn't trust her legs. She lived further from school than I did. She was smaller than me, which made it easy to catch her each time she swooned. We were both in shock, and I was glad for the company. What we had just heard made no sense. Why would anyone shoot President Kennedy?

I deposited my friend on her front steps and continued towards home. The streets were uncharacteristically quiet except for the seagulls. Everyone was inside watching TV.

I was surprised to find my father camped out in front of the television when I walked in our front door, his shoulders rigid, oblivious to anything but the news. I paused mid-step, transfixed by a single tear sliding down his cheek. The unimaginable had happened. John Fitzgerald Kennedy was dead. I didn't know heroes could die or grown men cry.

The wallpaper blurred with my own tears. I'd been strong until this moment. I heard the swish of tires on asphalt, a squealing gull, the heavy step of my ultra-pregnant mother in the other room, and the ticking of our mantle clock.

I was confused and off-balance. Life as I knew it was over and yet it continued to tick along. We would eat dinner, go to bed, and on Monday return to school, yet nothing would feel the same.

Three days later, the whole family went house hunting. I remember all of us silently transfixed in a stranger's living room as JFK's funeral procession paraded across her TV screen, united in our grief.

His horse-drawn coffin was followed by a symbolic riderless horse. Black Jack was distractingly magnificent, picked because even at sixteen, he couldn't be ridden. He jigged down the street, fighting the man with his hand on the bridle every step of the way, a pair of tall riding boots set backwards into the stirrups. The black gelding fought his handler the same way I fought to contain my emotions as I tried to make sense of what had happened.

In the weeks to follow I aged a million years. I found myself questioning things I'd always known for certain. I caught myself pausing before jumping off the boardwalk or looking over my shoulder before climbing into forbidden places. I saw the same hesitations in my brothers and our friends.

The assassination had damaged our confidence, and in the coming years I came to know that this was the day a whole generation lost its innocence. Up to now, I'd believed in the infallible protection of our leaders, but with a single bullet I realized I was on my own.

Michael's Birth Day November 27, 1963

It was just before Thanksgiving that Michael was born. Five minutes 'till midnight November 27, 1963 at Sitkim Hospital in Neptune City, in Neptune Township and five days after JFK's assassination.

We had been in the process of buying a home and had been looking at a farm house, just days before he was born. I remember us standing in the owner's living room, silently watching JFK's funeral with the homeowner. John and I both cried the day Kennedy was assassinated. John never cried, but he cried then.

We were getting ready to have Nana over for Thanksgiving which was a departure from the norm as most family holidays were held at her house. But Thanksgiving this year was so close to my due date that we decided to stay close to home.

John didn't want a turkey this time so he got three Cornish hens. I was stuffing these little hens for Thanksgiving when I began getting labor pains. John had already eaten dinner and was out teaching class at Monmouth College.

So, I needed a ride because John had the car. I called the police, and they sent a car over. I don't recall who came over to watch the kids; I just remember I was stranded. It may have been Margie, the woman who cleaned our house.

This policeman had children that went to the same school as the kids so his kids knew our kids. We got to the hospital and went into the waiting room and were waiting for someone to come and take care of me. While we waited, the officer and I continued the conversation we'd started on the drive over about the school. He wasn't satisfied with the school and was planning to move his children to Saint Dennis.

Finally, I said, "Oh, when is this nurse going to come around?" He immediately got up to see and she said, "Oh, I thought the pains had stopped because you were having such a long conversation!" and had gone on to help other people first.

I went to the labor room, which is where you went until time for delivery, and then you went to the delivery room. John was able to get out of class and come to the hospital while I was in the labor room.

I remember in the labor room I was really uncomfortable, and I was just shaking all over because that's what pain did to me. They said they could give me a little something that wouldn't make me feel like sleeping. I think I always had this much pain when in labor. Whether I was in pain or very cold, I would get the shakes. The nurses couldn't work with me the way I was shaking, so they gave me something for the pain.

After Michael was born, the nurse said, "You're husband is out here waiting for you, would you like to see him?" This nurse was so dear. She was older and had a motherly disposition. She took me down the hall, and it was very quiet. When John saw us coming, he came rushing towards me. "I'm so happy that you are doing so well!" he said. I can still picture the stillness of that hospital hall, John's eyes filled with so much love, and the smile of that motherly nurse. His caresses were so tender and loving; I was completely enveloped in his love.

Michael, John, and Joe

I hadn't seen the baby yet and didn't know if it was a boy or a girl. John told me we had had a beautiful boy and walked back to the room with me, holding my hand all the way and saying, "You just go to sleep." And then he went back home to take care of the other kids. Joe was only two years old then and Camille was only nine.

We brought Michael home a few days later. My mother had come down to help care for us, the four young children and newborn number five. When I walked into the house, everything was wonderful! Mother had hot food cooking on the stove, and everything was so organized. She had everything set up and was ready to take care of me. I told her "You are the eye of the hurricane!"

And then there was Hortense, who used to come over to help with the housework. She was a big black woman, very jolly and did an excellent job when we couldn't get Margie. Camille loved her, and she was great with everyone. How she loved Michael!

"How could anyone not want their babies?" Hortense would say. Michael would be on his tummy, but he wouldn't want to go to sleep because there was so much going on. He never cried because all the other children were running around, giving him so much to think about.

When people ask me, "How do you do it?" I tell them "Well, the more you have, the more help you have from the others!"

West Long Branch, New Jersey 1964-1970

It took a couple of tries to find our new home. John's brother Frank said, "That looks like a slum," about the first house we looked at. But when we saw the house at 64 Hollywood Avenue, we didn't get that feeling at all. I remember thinking the balcony made it look like Noah's Ark.

Camille: According to a pamphlet put out by the West Long Branch Historical Society in 2000, the house on Hollywood Avenue was part of a colony of summer rentals for the wealthy developed in the late 1800's. "Norwood Park, An Exclusive Summer Cottage Colony," was comprised of twenty large, two and three-story Victorians, a casino, stables, and race track a mile from the beach.

Cousin Barbara (Grace) and the house at 64 Hollywood Avenue

The cottage at 64 Hollywood Avenue was added in 1924, a larger version of the original cottages. It lost its third floor to a fire in the fifties and was re-roofed as a two-story home. Even without the third floor, the house was enormous by our standards with 4,104 square feet of living space and a wrap-around porch. It had four bedrooms, two and a half bathrooms, three fireplaces, a ballroom, dining room, three sun porches, and a couple of balconies. The house sold for $373,500 in 2015.

After we moved in, I was thrilled to discover horses on the other side of the hedge across the street. We were just a couple of blocks from Monmouth College where my father taught, and a twenty-minute walk from the beach. On weekends, we swam in the heated indoor pool at Monmouth or attended concerts. I recall seeing Bruce Springsteen with Steel Mill on campus.

Most of the other cottages were inhabited by big Catholic families, so we had plenty of friends. Many of our neighbors were school mates at Saint Jerome's Catholic School, less than a mile away. One of the fifteen climbing trees in our yard was tall enough for us to see the top of the *school. There were enough kids in the neighborhood that we were able to throw together baseball and football games in the spacious back yards on a whim.*

On City Island, we didn't have all those bedrooms, but we did in Avon, and from then on we always wanted to have a big house. I think it was John's friends, the Brewers, who lived on Ocean Avenue, who recommended the house. They only wanted $17,400, and John stipulated they redo the porches. It was such a thrill moving into that West Long Branch house. $17,400! Can you imagine buying a home like that?

One of our favorite restaurants while we lived in West Long Branch was Freddie's Pizzeria. We usually took the kids there for birthdays, but left them home when we went there to celebrate our anniversary. Then John would play a song for me on their juke box, something about a husband coming home to his wife, and singing her praises because she always made sure there was a good meal on the table, and the baby was playing nice.

Johnny noticed a fruit truck going by in West Long Branch. I said "You hail them down and you pick out what you want." And Nana gave us her fruit basket. And that's still there on top of the buffet in the farm house. The very same fruit basket Camille would arrange for Thanksgiving. I think both the basket and the table came from the Stone Church. They had a big sale at least once a year. John would take some of the kids and go, while I stayed home with the baby.

When we lived in West Long Branch, the kids spent a lot of time at Nana's in Atlantic Highlands, a twenty-minute drive away. Camille played Nana's piano that stood on the windowed front porch. One day she said, "You know when you blend two notes to make a chord, it's a lot like mixing two colors to make a third color."

The boys didn't play the piano at Nana's much; they were too busy running around the neighborhood. Nana said, "I get so aggravated trying to get them all together to come in for a meal, and then I feel so bad the next day I spoil them to death!"

John didn't like it at Monmouth College even though he earned more money than he did at Saint Vincent in Latrobe. He said the administration was "chicken shit."

Camille: The Vietnam War had the country astir, especially the peace-loving hippies. We called ourselves freaks. I remember cutting classes one day to take the train to New York City with some classmates. I was probably a sophomore, so it would have been 1969 or 1970. We were inspired by the dynamic speakers at the peace rallies in Washington Square in Greenwich Village and brought the peace movement back to school with us.

I knew my father shared my sentiments and was proud of him for that. Towards the end of the school year, he resigned from his job because, as I heard it told, he encouraged his students to protest against a general who was speaking at Monmouth College. I heard something about marshmallows being thrown on the stage. Although he searched for another teaching post in New Jersey, and then New York, nothing was coming up. Nana said he'd never get another teaching job in New Jersey because he'd been blackballed.

Finally, he got a job at Shippensburg State Teacher's College in central Pennsylvania, two hundred miles away. Dad called it the armpit of the universe and I was inclined to agree. It broke my heart to leave all my good friends behind. I think it broke Nana's and Dad's hearts, too. My parents threw me a sweet sixteen birthday party at our big house on Hollywood Avenue. I didn't want the evening to end because I couldn't bear to say goodbye.

The chip on my shoulder must have shown because I had a super hard time fitting in at my new school. Only the outcasts would grant me access to their friendship. For that I was grateful. However, it started me down a bad path, and it took me ten or fifteen years to get back on track. Even so, I was super proud of my father for standing true to his beliefs and wouldn't have wanted him to keep his mouth shut just to stay at Monmouth College.

After we moved to Shippensburg, real estate went up. By the time we sold the house in West Long Branch, it was worth double that. I think we sold it for $32k. Meanwhile, we rented it to a woman who had a lot of cats. We'd left the piano there, and when we went back for it, the piano smelled so bad I didn't even want to bring it to Pennsylvania. But they'd made this new stuff, a spray that completely took the smell away without leaving any smell of its own behind, so we sprayed it down and moved it to Shippensburg.

James' Birth Day July 11, 1965

Just hours before James was born, we adults were invited to the Barnett's, our neighbors down the street in West Long Branch. They invited the Hopkins, too for drinks and salty things at their house.

I was so tempted by the ginger ale. When you're pregnant, you hold the water in, so I tried not to drink too much and was thirsty all the time. To check to see if you have too much water in your system, you press your fingers into your leg against the shin bone. Normally, the indentation comes right up, but when you're holding too much water that indentation stays. My father had that problem with water staying in because he had kidney disease, so my mother was always checking his legs for that.

So, I just had a half a cup of ginger ale and two or three peanuts, and we had a real nice time. We were talking about the O'Dwyers who were invited, too but couldn't make it. Mrs. Barnett said, "Oh, I envy her because every night when we're just starting to eat and I look over, her kitchen light is off already. I don't know how late this was, about 8:00 or 9:00.

We returned home, and baby Michael woke up, so I sat in the rocking chair with him and thought, "I feel so uncomfortable," which wasn't the case with that nice, comfortable chair, and then I realized I was starting to get contractions.

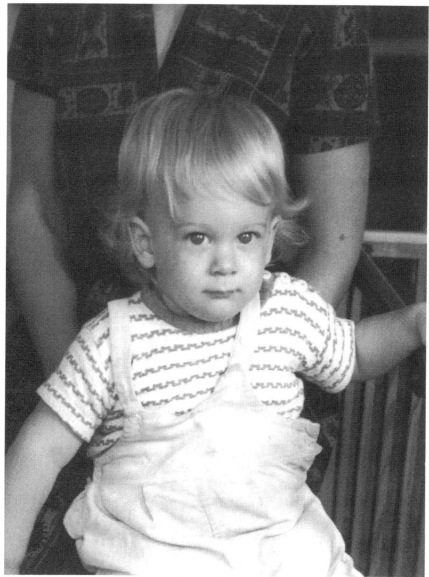

Baby James

I don't know if Camille was still up or if we woke her, but we asked her to take care of the kids so John could take me to the hospital. She was very happy to do that and excited that we were going to have another baby.

So I went there and they gave me a spinal, and it seems it didn't take very long before James was born, sometime after midnight. I was very happy. I couldn't really hold the baby because they tell you that if you sit up, you'll get a headache so I had to lie there for eight hours. When I first held James, I was taken by his big beautiful eyes.

I got phlebitis, an inflammation of the veins while I was in the hospital. It looked like a bruise and really hurt bad. When the nurse came in she said, "You should have the doctor look at that" and when the doctor saw it, he said it was a deep vein.

Deep veins are dangerous because they mean you have a blood clot which can go up into your lungs and kill you. So, the nurses worked night and day, putting hot packs on it every twenty minutes to get me back on my feet. When I left the hospital they told me to continue with the hot packs.

I came home in three days this time, and I didn't have anybody to help me because my mother couldn't come. I talked to Camille on the phone from the hospital, and she wanted to help. So I gave her a list of what to get at the store and she went on her bike, and got all of those things.

When John brought me home from the hospital, Bobby was playing outside the house on the tricycle, the one with the big front wheel. He was about six years old, and when he saw us drive up, he got so excited! He saw us getting out of the car with the baby and yelled, "Mommy's here! With the baby!"

When I walked inside the house, it looked so beautiful to me. The family had all gotten everything cleaned, John bought a new floral tablecloth, and Camille had shopped for everything I'd asked for. And John (he was such a good cook) already had dinner made.

It was just such a happy moment to be walking into my house with a brand new baby, and seeing all the kids. Everyone was so happy! When you're in the hospital, everything is all white, there's no color. And then when you get home, you realize what a beautiful home you have!

So everything was taken care of except for a surface vein which wasn't dangerous, but which was very painful. It just burned so bad. They said take sitz baths in witch hazel for twenty minutes.

I was talking with Ann Howe on the phone, and she asked how everything was going. I said, "Everything's fine except I don't have anybody here to help this time, and I need to get off my feet. Being on my feet so much has made this surface vein sore, and it's getting more uncomfortable by the minute." And she said she could get off work and come stay with me. She came and slept in the upstairs sun porch room with James in his bassinette and took care of him all night long, giving him his bottle. And during the day, she took care of the children as well!

Ann said she was so happy to be with the family. She helped me so much, that between her and the witch hazel, I was able to recover. Meanwhile, I still cooked. I had two chairs in the kitchen that I would put my feet up on while I prepared dinner, and we were able to manage.

On the last day before Ann left, John took us all out to Asbury Park. We put James in the little car seat and went down to Carvel for ice cream cones for a treat. It was so much fun! Camille and Johnny were sitting in the back seat, and the wind was blowing ice cream droplets all over the car. Ann and I were giggling so and trying to buck up against the wind, laughing so hard that the kids were getting irritated, saying "Get in the car and close the windows!"

After Ann went home, I saw Dr. Federici (another one of our neighbors) and he said, "That's the fastest I've ever seen phlebitis heal!"

The first night on my own, I took James downstairs and gave him his bottle and, as always, sat there in my spot in the kitchen. It was so peaceful, and I could hear things outside. It was early morning when the birds start in, and then they stop for a while, kind of a false dawn.

When I got baby James back upstairs, I didn't put him back to bed right away. Instead, I took him out onto the balcony and the stars were shining. I could see him in the starlight and oh, his eyes were so big looking up at me. He looks like Mighty Mouse, I thought. He had a beautiful chiseled face and even the new mother superior said, "He's so beautiful for a boy, his face is so perfect, as if it were chiseled." James had the biggest eyes of all my children.

When I told my mother about baby James, she said, "The way you're talking about him, so full of wonder and love, you'd never know he was your sixth baby and not your first."

Next thing you know I was giving James his bath while the kids were playing outside. And Bobby just loved coming up and seeing James in his bassinette. And I made up this song:

What happened, what happened?
There used to be not any
But now there are so many
What happened, what happened
How did these dears come to be?
From whe-ere, from whe-ere?
These loves surely came from somewhere
The sweet smiles and pure eyes
And I love them so much
Now I know, now I know
One day I think heaven overflowed
And spilled them right into our house.

I had gotten stuck on the line "The sweet smiles," but Bobby rescued me by adding "and pure eyes." I sang this song at our fiftieth anniversary, and I'm pretty sure Charity, Johnny's daughter, remembers it.

One time, Camille was with me in the room. I had just finished changing James. I realized that, every time something dropped or any quick sound was made, James used to laugh his chipmunk laugh. All I had to do was suck my teeth when I was eating strawberries to get him to laugh. I told Camille about his laugh. So, she tried it, and sure enough he laughed, and we all laughed and laughed.

James kept this laugh, and when we were visiting Camille and Bob in Virginia years later, and listening to old audio tapes, Jim's chipmunk laugh came out.

Parenthood

John and I worked together at naming the kids. We named Camille Louise; Camille after Grandpa's sister, a woman who was so helpful to her mother that Nana used to say, "She's a saint," and after my mother's sister, my Aunt Louise. Louise is my middle name, too. I used to call baby Camille "Bunny."

1961 Camille's first communion with Bobby and Johnny at Nana's

We named John Roderick after John and my father. We named Robert Joseph after my Uncle Bob and John's favorite uncle on his father's side, Uncle Jody. I used to affectionately call him "Bobby Robin."

Joseph Peter was named after John's Uncle Jody. Peter is John's middle name, too. When Jody was a baby, our neighbor came over to see if her daughters were playing at our house. I picked up Joe and said, "Little Jody Peter," and he looked so nice to this woman, it made her want another child.

We named Michael Phillip after Michael the archangel and my cousin, Michael Dolan. I was reading the bible at the time and was really interested in the saints, and I thought the two names sounded nice together. James was James Matthew because we liked Saint Matthew. I used to call him "Jamie Jame James."

Janice, James, and Michael

Once when I was out for a walk with the kids (it was All Saint's Day, just after Halloween) we met a woman and she asked Camille, "How do you feel with all these boys?" Camille answered, "Oh, I feel like a queen."

~*~

Bobby would balance his slippers on each other, so they didn't take up so much room under his bed. When we lived in West Long Branch, I'd walk into a room and see these slippers piled up on top of each other.

~*~

Our children really all looked alike. I remember when we went to Roland Labs in Shippensburg, the principle remarked at how much Joe, Michael and James resembled each other.

~*~

When John and I came out to Pennsylvania in 1969 to look for a place, my mother came down to stay with the kids in West Long Branch. "Joe," she said, "My goodness!" He had gotten the Three Musketeers to arrange their sleeping toys on the top of the door. Joe, Michael, and James, I always called them The Three Musketeers because they were always together. When my mother pushed the door open, stuffed animals came tumbling down on her. She was easily startled like I am.

One time, my mother was waiting in line for something, and there was this little Jewish man, and he had dropped his keys. She cried out "Oh my dear!" as he bent over to pick them up. He looked up at her and said, "Madame?!" questioning the endearment. She was so embarrassed!

The three musketeers, Michael, James, and Joe

All six of our kids had the chicken pox. Mothers are jacks of all trade and masters of all, doctors, plumbers and so on. I was never mechanically inclined, but boy did I learn fast. I had to deal with things that had fallen apart and had to be fixed.

~*~

"A man works from sun to sun, a women's work is never done." Women's work is a different kind of work. We are the heart, and men are the head. If someone calls or comes to the door, we try to fit it in. We have a lot of heart-related interruptions, which is why we have endurance. That's why God made us that way. The men seem to die off early.

Camille

Camille wet the bed until she was seven. I asked Lil Brown for advice, and she suggested setting an alarm. I told Camille "Tell yourself you're gonna stay dry until the alarm goes off." That worked until she was twelve or thirteen, and then she started again. And then I had to wash everything and said, "Please dear, put the alarm on." That went on for a year, maybe two at the most.

Camille used to be the centurion, the guard who watched out the door to see if everything was alright with her brothers, and if it wasn't, if they'd started fighting or something, she'd report it to me so I could turn off the stove and go out.

She made up games, too. I suggested she get her brothers to play with the blocks and she came up with a game she called "Peek House." She'd make a block house with a little hole in top, put something in there, then have them come over and guess what it was. Another game was "Guess what's up my nose," in which they would turn their face and sneak the bottom of a pencil or something along their nose so it would appear to be coming out of their nostril.

John would sing to Bobby, who had big nostrils "Blow your nose, blow your nose. There's a booger in there as big as a bear, so blow your nose!"

Cauliflower was Camille's favorite vegetable when she was a child. The night before she had her tonsils out, I made her favorite meal of fried hamburger, mashed potatoes, and cauliflower, which she would stir up all together. She loved it that way!

I sent Camille to school with sandwiches made of all kinds of leftovers; lentils and different vegetables. One of her friends always had leftover steak in her sandwiches, and Camille envied her so. But her friend envied the variety Camille had in her lunch, so they traded. Camille couldn't imagine what she saw in her leftover sandwiches.

I used to get collard greens in a can and add them to my lentil soup. By themselves they didn't taste like much, but with the lentils they tasted alright.

Baby Camille and Grandpa Frank

Camille: my best friend, Franny's mother was a nurse, so she got me and Fran involved in the Candy Striper program at the hospital when we were about thirteen years old. We'd walk the mile to the hospital in our red and white striped uniforms, and do whatever they needed us to do.

Camille's Candy Striper friends said one day, "Hey, let's surprise your mother and clean this whole downstairs." I said, "Just when I start worrying about the kids and drugs, they go and do something so nice. They just become angels! You know, age is a revelation."

The kids could smoke out on the porch. We couldn't have smoke in the house with John's asthma. Billy Shuda (he lived a couple of blocks over and went to school with Camille) he just smelled like burnt rope when he came over.

One day when Camille was around fourteen she decided to clean out her closet, and I saw all these pictures that she drew on these big tablets in her waste basket. I retrieved them, and when I showed them to John's cousin, Tommy Russell (he was a graphic artist), he said, "Look at this horse, it's going sixty miles an hour!"

Camille and Bob Armantrout at their wedding with Janice, brother Bobby and his wife, Debbee, and brother James - July 31, 1994

Johnny

Camille and Johnny on Nana's swing set

Camille: My brother Johnny works with developmentally challenged people, a source of great amusement to him. His clients are unapologetically candid, he says, crude and refreshingly unfiltered. He likes people, it's as simple as that.

John is deeply talented but has put his creative career aside in favor of enriching our parents' sunset years. Although his photography should be legendary, he never toots his own horn. He understands light like no one else. His creative eye unerringly homes in on the essence of a scene. He's done a lot of studio portraits, many of them pro bono and has an uncanny way of teasing out his subject's inner beauty.

You would never know that John suffers from migraines and back pain. At family events he works the room with tripod and cameras, mining for gold. Looking over photographs from our youngest brother's wedding, we're captured in candid enjoyment at round tables laden with food. John is missing. He's behind the camera, and I realize, has been on his feet the entire time. It's all right, he tells me, it's the editing not the standing that bothers his back.

John has a gaggle of grandkids and they crawl all over him, loving his attention, stealing his glasses. They call him Grandpa Basil. They make movies together, sophisticated ones with plots and multiple camera angles. The kids are great, flawlessly in character but I know how much behind-the-scenes patience it takes to pull this off. How John does this after a full time job and running our parents around, is beyond me. Surely he must pick the days between headaches, although I can't imagine they are easily scheduled.

I was a pampered only child, regarded as miracle incarnate by my parents, until their next miracle appeared. Like many first-borns I felt dethroned, but quickly shifted gears after realizing I now owned a real-life doll baby.

We were the perfect two-child family for three years. There's a lovely photo of us, sitting on the stone steps outside our home in Norvelt, Pennsylvania, my mother beaming, my father slightly distracted by the camera timer, Johnny and I unaccustomed to sitting still.

Camille and Johnny - Easter 1959

    Dad immortalized our relationship in another photograph. Johnny and I are in our Easter best, he in a jaunty sailboat shirt and me clutching my hatbox. I've got a firm grip on my little brother with my other hand. My attitude is doting and overbearing, his response unabashedly trusting. Johnny bought into my wisdom until he was old enough to question my authority, after which he was wise enough make it appear he still trusted my judgement.

Once we were playing on ice, and it began to break. I watched in horror as Johnny began floating out into Hudson Bay. "Jump!" I shrieked, and he stepped off into the knee-deep water without hesitation. Another time we were playing with friends, rolling around on their lawn, when the younger girl picked up a huge rock and dropped it on Johnny's forehead. Her big sister fetched her mother, and I ran all the way home to tell mine. Mom flew out the door, leaving me in charge. Terrified he was dying; I prayed the rosary again and again until she brought him home, alive.

John jokes about the incident, "I think she was trying to impress me," he says. He is one of those guys who sees the funny in everything. John is also a gifted mimic, easily assuming personas to illustrate a joke. Even his complaints turn into jokes. We talk on the phone after dinner sometimes, laughing until tears flow and my jaw muscles seize up. "Remember that kid," he'll begin, and I know I'm in for a good one.

When we were in our thirties, John and I visited our grandmother's home. "Let's pretend we're little kids again," he suggested, picking up my hand. "We would walk like this," he said, taking a tiny little step towards the terrace above the vegetable garden. Off we went, climbing the concrete steps, navigating an enormous world and we small as toddlers. My eyes shone.

Life without John would be boring and burdensome, yet I take his presence for granted. It seems like he's always been there, shouldering the hard work while making me feel big, picking up the pieces and joking about it. He touches many lives in profound ways without making anyone feel indebted. My little brother is bigger than me and has been for a long time. But don't let him catch you saying that because he'll defend his big sister's honor with sincere fervor to the end.

Bobby

Camille: Few of us make it to adulthood without suffering a few setbacks, but not all of us are lucky enough to have someone fighting hard to pull us through. When Bobby Illo was at George Junior Republic, Mom wasn't going to stop until she found a way to help him rise above his circumstances.

Pilot Bobby

Bobby hadn't exactly been looking for trouble when he got caught returning a 'borrowed' delivery truck. He had merely been trying to help our neighbor Julia's visiting nephew. She had taken in her nephew Wally because his family in Baltimore couldn't manage him. While she didn't like the idea, she couldn't refuse, and hoped she could get Wally into the Mercersburg Academy.

Bobby

Whereas Wally didn't drive, Bobby did. Wally was getting pretty homesick for his friends in Baltimore, but he didn't know how to drive. He suggested to Bobby that they

127

borrow a delivery truck and make the two-hour trip, after which Bobby could bring the truck back before the merchants even realized it was missing. Bobby agreed, and the rest is history. As penance, Bobby was shipped off to George Junior Republic, a boarding school that specialized in at "at-risk" kids. What happened to Wally? As far as Mom recalls, nothing happened to him because he wasn't driving.

Bobby was doing so well at George Junior that Mom decided to try and give him a reward by obtaining permission for him to resume his flying lessons. She soon found out that simply asking wasn't enough. Undeterred, Mom said, "I'm a fighter."

After speaking with a doctor who happened to have a pilot's license, Mom called the FAA, and they wrote a letter of recommendation to George Junior. She got the school to write a letter, too. The letters did the trick, and Bobby was allowed his lessons. In this way, Mom helped Bobby to soar above his situation.

~*~

Camille: Bobby and I drove from Shippensburg to Denver when he was eighteen and I was twenty-two. I'll never forget how everyone stopped chewing, when we announced our plans at my parents' dinner table. But, he was of age, and we were both sure he was ready to leave the nest.

We took turns driving, talking and singing to pass the time, in one of those spent cars I'd gotten for cheap at auction, probably the burgundy Pontiac sedan, ignoring the threat of engine failure, or blow-outs. The Texas panhandle was a particularly godforsaken stretch. It was dark, but we could see lights up ahead, which raised our hopes that we would soon reach a town with a motel. But time stood still, and we didn't reach those lights for hours.

Bobby's good humor steadied us, and saw us through. Years later, I listened to the tape we made driving across the panhandle, and realized how mature Bobby was. If you didn't know better, you would think I was the petulant teen, and Bobby was the emotionally-mature twenty-two year old.

We rented an apartment in Aurora from a nice older couple. Our landlord was a race track announcer at Centennial Downs, and he helped me get a job grooming horses. Bobby found a gig shagging cars. We took turns sleeping on the couch, the only other bed being the floor. We'd lay there and talk about everything until one of us fell asleep. It was like a slumber party every night.

When the trainers loaded up the horses for Santé Fe, I hopped in with them. I felt a little bad for abandoning my younger brother, but I wasn't worried. I knew he could take care of himself just as well as I could, and maybe even better.

Joe

Joe loved the ocean so much that when he was a toddler on City Island, he would go into the water, laughing and laughing, wading in deeper and deeper until we had to pull him out. I'd have his hand, but he just kept pulling me in further. He was happiest when the water was up over his head, and he was laughing all the way.

Joe loved to dig holes in the back yard, and he'd be covered in dirt from head to toe. Aunt Kathy came over when we lived on City Island, and when she saw Joe she said, "He's a very dirty little baby, isn't he?" Every night, I'd give him a bath and wash it all off.

Kathy and Frank lived in New York, so she'd come often and spend the whole day when she was pregnant with Mark. Nana had given them the acre next door, and they were having a house built on it. They built their house for $17,000 and customized it with a bedroom downstairs for Kathy's mother, Mrs. Hugart.

When Joe was just a year old or so (he could walk), we'd go to Nana's for the weekend. One weekend, he was wearing a yellow sleeper, the kind with the feet in, and he disappeared. Nana called either the Fire or Police Department because we couldn't find him anywhere. It wasn't that he was angry at anybody or didn't want to be with us; he just had so much interest in everything, and would just walk on down the road.

And then we got a phone call from the people down at the Stone Church. It was a Saturday morning. The Episcopal priest and his wife had been to a party the night before and were trying to sleep in. As she told Aunt Kathy, "Here I am all hung over, and I look out my window and there's a baby walking around!"

In Avon, I had to tether him in the back yard to keep him from running down the street to the beach. "Mom!" Camille said, "That's supposed to be against the law!" But I couldn't keep my eye on him with all the cooking and cleaning that went with running a home with four other children. This was after he chased a beach ball all the way down to Belmar. I sent Camille back home to call the police and she learned they had found Joe. But when she returned to me, she decided not to tell me right away, as a prank.

I didn't have to do this with everyone, but after the older kids ran in a couple of times saying, "Joe's run out of the yard!" I felt I had no choice. When Michael got to be that age, I prepared to put him on the tether but he protested, "No, I don't need it! I don't want to run out of the yard. Just try me!" So I gave him a chance and kept an eye on him from the kitchen window. Sure enough, he never left the yard.

On City Island, Camille and Johnny would run next door to Lil's or the movie theater. But they never went any further. They loved playing with the Brown's adopted son, Louie. Sometimes Rossie, their oldest son would play with them in the Brown's backyard. I remember talking with Tommy about how good our children were, "We don't deserve kids this good!"

~*~

John's brother, Frank, and I were talking about guardian angels. He wasn't sure he believed in that, but I said, "Well if you had six kids you'd either have to believe in guardian angels or have eyes in the back of your head." "I suppose!" he said, thoughtfully.

~*~

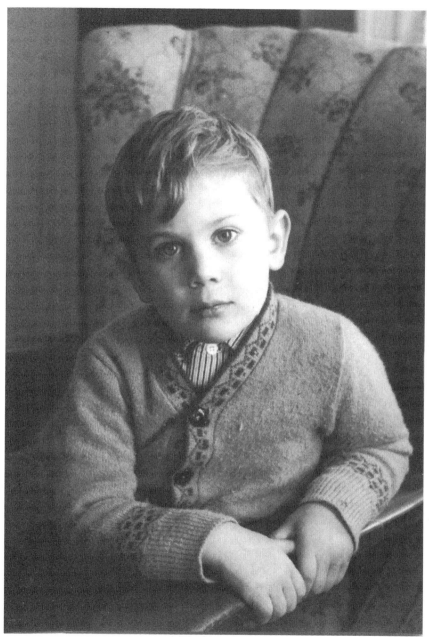

Little Napoleon

In West Long Branch, we'd go down to the beach, and one day Joe was digging in the sand. The kids liked to dig down deep until they hit water because that sand stuck together better for making sand castles.

Joe was a little young to be making sandcastles, but he could dig holes. So he got in the spirit of things, and kept digging deeper and deeper. Until the lifeguard came over and told him, "Hey, fill that hole up." And little Joe, probably no more than three years old, looked up at the lifeguard with a real pouty and determined look and said, "No!" and kept right on digging.

That's how forceful Joe was. I used to call him my little Napoleon. Here was this big strong man with a thick belt around his waist with I don't remember what on it, looking so official, and Joe refused to listen to him.

So, I came running down from our blanket and said, "I'll get him out!" and to Joe, "Joe, you fill that hole up right now!" And he did it. The lifeguard looked dumfounded. The kids always obeyed me.

By now, the other lifeguard had come over to see what the trouble was, and seeing that the problem had been solved asked the first lifeguard, "How did you make him fill up the hole?" "His mother asked him and he did it!" he said, amazed.

~*~

When we were in Shippensburg, Nana brought us a plant, and we put it in the window. I hoped it wouldn't die, but Joe made sure it didn't. He used the little watering can Nana had brought and kept after it every day.

Rachel Steck, one of our neighbors had all these beautiful plants in her back yard. One day she brought over a load of marigolds, and told Joe how to plant them; which he did, along the fence outside the dining room window, so I could see them from my place at the table.

Joe definitely had a green thumb, and so he didn't stop with marigolds. He went on to dig up a plot for a vegetable garden behind the garage, beyond the row of marigolds.

When we lived out at the farm, he heard about Youth Conservation Corps up at King's Gap up on the mountain. High school kids would put their names on the list if they wanted to do that sort of work, helping maintain the parks. Joe loved working with the Corps. Up there, you'll see his name engraved on plaques at the different parks where he worked.

He'd take me up there in the fall to see the beautiful foliage. The last time we went, we spoke with a forest ranger and found out he knew the forester who had been there when Joe was working with the Corps. Joe also kept the trees pruned out at the farm, with John's permission, of course. So, that's why Joe wanted to major in Forestry at Penn State.

Pope Paul II and Joseph, Christmas Day 1986

We called him Jody until we moved to Shippensburg and he found out the little girl next door's name was Jodi. "That's awful, naming your son a girl's name!" "No," I protested, "Her name is spelled Jodi and yours is the male version, Jody." But he wouldn't hear of it, so I asked him,

"Well, what do you want to be called?" He said, "Call me Joe" After that we called him Joe until he became a priest and went by Father Joseph.

When he lived in Shippensburg, Joe liked to go down to the corner store and buy these Pez candies, fruit flavored lozenges. He got these every day at Bigler's. I took Joe to the dentist, and for the first time, one of our kids had cavities. He came back with eight cavities! Our children never ate candy and their teeth were really good, no one ever had any cavities until Joe.

I told him, "You've got to stop doing that! Just eat dessert, and no candy." But I guess he overdid it, because after we moved out to the farm, he started refusing desert. Then he started having headaches, so I took him to the doctor in Hershey. Turned out, now he had low blood sugar. The remedy was sugar cubes, so I bought some and I told him to take one every once in a while.

He put a sign on his door "10 cents apiece for sugar cubes. Money goes to Mommy to pay for my trip to France." He had another sign, "Toyland is open," and on the other side it said, "Toyland is closed." I'd hear the kids say, "Oh boy, Toyland is open!"

He was the boss over Michael and James. Boy did they miss it when Joe went on that retreat and spent the summer at Aunt Ibby's in Utah. All of the kids went out there to Ibby and Sergene's ranch, and they paid Joe to work there.

When Joe was going to college, he majored in Forestry. He always loved plants, beginning with our backyard on City Island where he dug in the dirt, loving the earth and all the plants and bugs that were around.

Camille: Joe was called to the priesthood and asked to be sent to a diocese close to Yosemite National Park in California. As a Catholic priest, Reverend Joseph Illo travels extensively and has met many deeply devout people, including Mother Teresa and Saint Pope John Paul II.

Joseph kneeling beside Mother Teresa

Michael

When John used to get home from college for the day, he'd come back and relax in the dining room. And Michael would wake up from his nap. John called him Pinky because he had a rosy face from sleeping just like I had when I first woke up. And I always called him Pink Heart.

Michael and James

I went out to see James and Lupe, his girlfriend in California, and stayed with Lupe in her apartment near Saint Ignatius Press. We took naps one afternoon, and when I woke up, James said, "Your face is all pink and rosy."

When I was a teenager, my girlfriend's family invited me to Rochester. We took naps, and when we came down for supper, I remember my face was all pink.

When the boy's father saw my pink cheeks he said, "Well, someone's been to the powder room!" As far as he was concerned, I had made myself up to please his son, and he wouldn't believe anything different.

One day John said, "There's something wrong with Pinky. He can't talk!" We couldn't figure out what was wrong, but he was holding a Tinkertoy stick and trying to tell us something. We took him to the doctor, and it turned out he had fallen on that stick, and it had poked a big a sore on his tongue.

Camille: In West Long Branch, my parents turned the sun porch off the dining room into a play room. The room faced west with a complete wall of square-paned windows reaching from wainscoting to ceiling. We kept those windows open spring, fall, and winter (no air conditioning in those days) so it had enough ventilation for me to use my oil paints. I can picture that room whenever I smell linseed oil. There were only two ways out of the room, to sit on a window ledge and jump to the ground, or push open the heavy door. The top half of the door was glass, which made it easy for my mother to keep an eye on us from the kitchen.

Johnny and Connie Mayer were in the porch room and Michael was on the other side of the door. And there were bees in there, and the bees were making a beeline towards Johnny and Connie. The two of them ran to the big door with the big, glass window. The door was closed, Johnny's hand went right through the glass, breaking it, and a big piece fell and sliced open Michael's temple.

Johnny, Michael, the neighbor, Connie, Bobby, Joe, and Camille
West Long Branch

It was a weekend, because John was home. We called the new doctor who just was moving in, and he said, "Get a cold rag from the refrigerator, and hold it tight against the wound and have your husband drop him here." When we got there, he said Michael was going to be alright because it cut into a fleshy spot, not bone. Michael had a favorite wind-up toy that played "Sing a Song of Sixpence," that he serenaded the doctor with while he stitched. The doctor put in ten or twelve stitches, and told me "I didn't know you'd be able to take seeing all that blood. So many mothers pass out when they see that much blood. You're a strong woman!"

Camille: I remember being in the room with Johnny, our panic over the monster bee, which was probably just a carpenter bee, our rush to the closed door with Johnny in the lead, and in slow motion, his hand missing the waist-high door knob, and plunging through the glass. The window broke into huge pieces, all with a central point where Johnny's hand had gone through, and one tumbled to the left where baby Michael was bouncing in one of those canvas seats with springs attached to a metal frame. An edge caught the side of his face and sliced a neat six-inch path. Just laid it open.

Michael jumping over his leg 1976

When Michael lived at the Molly Pitcher in Carlisle, he hung his carton of eggs out the window because he didn't have a refrigerator. He must have remembered me telling him that when my mother and I lived in South Hill, we didn't have a refrigerator, so we used to hang frozen orange juice and everything else out the window. We were in the top apartment, and Jeanette and Bob lived in one of the other apartments on the hill below us.

My mother paid his rent. He wanted to live on his own, and I'd come over and bring him food for the week. He was eighteen and had quit school, but after he moved to Carlisle, he got his GED (high school equivalency certificate) and took the CAT bus (Capital Area Transit) to go to HACC, (Harrisburg Area Community College).

Michael would take the George Herriot books to school and the kids called him "bookie." He liked to read and walk, he'd get so interested in something he was reading that he'd lose his balance and fall down.

James

When James was old enough to ride on the little horse that Johnny used to play with in Norvelt, he fell and cut his chin on the brick steps out in front of the 64 Hollywood Avenue house, and I had to take him in for stitches. When I took him back a week or so later, the doctor said, "That's all healed!" I couldn't believe it, and I was delighted because it was a jagged and nasty wound. "Babies heal fast," the doctor added.

James earned the nickname "Snaggletooth," and he'd get so mad when the other kids called him that! As the youngest he sometimes used his teeth; it was the only way he could defend himself.

Jamie

Camille: My brother, Jamie, is easy-going, much like our Grandpa, Frank Illo. And, like Grandpa, he has a strong sense of family. Jamie has always made a point of connecting with aunts, uncles, and cousins, and wouldn't miss a family gathering. When he inherited Christina through his marriage to Kathryn, he embraced her as if she were his own daughter.

I was eleven when Jamie was born, and it was my privilege to help my mother care for him. I left home when Jamie was six, and didn't get the chance to know him in his adult phase until eighteen years later. Jamie knew, somehow, that I needed family around me that summer, so he drove out to Colorado and threw himself into my life for five weeks.

Uncle James, Amy, Molly, and Emily - Croaker Landing, Virginia 1996

We spent a lot of time at the barn where I kept my horse, Jesse. We were particularly fond of the barn cats. With his help, I started giving riding lessons. One day, we left the the barn in two cars, and when we arrived home, Jamie burst

142

out of his car. "Did you see that kitten?" he asked. "What kitten?" "The one that flew out of your wheel well! When you pulled onto the street from the barn!"

A few years later, I was having another rough patch, and Jamie came out again. He didn't make any grand announcements about rescuing me, but we both knew that's what he was doing. Jamie brought Mom out to Colorado when Bob and I got married, and drove her from Pennsylvania to Virginia to visit us and our three little girls when we celebrated all of our birthdays on July 4, 1996.

Jamie is so affable and low maintenance that he fits in everywhere, and is always welcome. It is through his efforts that our family stays connected and strong, and yet it's easy to miss the intention he puts into this. All we know is that he is there, and we're all having a great time!

Lost in New York City August, 1969

Camille: It was the weekend of the Woodstock Music and Art Fair, and I wanted to go more than anything. Some of my friends were going, but I was too young. However, I did make it to within two hundred miles of Woodstock because my mother took me and my brothers to visit her family in Ithaca that weekend. Port Authority was packed with hippies, and all I could do was gawk. I remember watching a wine bottle fall to the floor and shatter. The energy was incredible as people queued up for the trip to the music festival!

It was my first trip home to Ithaca in a long time. Camille had just turned fifteen. I led the caravan through Port Authority in New York City because I knew just where to go down to get the train. Camille was on the end, but Joe got away from her.

I went to the security office at Port Authority to report my missing child. The police said they had just received a call about a young boy. He was racing down the street crying, and was already in another precinct.

Camille had to go on alone with her other four brothers to Aunt Mabel and Uncle Emmet's while I stayed behind to find Joe. Mabel, my mother, and the rest met Camille and the boys up in Ithaca.

After I found Joe and made it up there, we settled in at Snyder's Tourist House (my mother had gotten us all rooms) right near the beautiful Cascadilla Gorge that ran through town. For dinner, my family wanted to take us over across a bridge to Just Joe's Italian Restaurant.

As soon as we started across the bridge, James climbed up on the railing. He always had really good balance, but here he was, only four years old, walking on the railing of the bridge. Aunt Mabel caught sight of him and said "We've got to keep an eye on these kids!"

I'll never forget how good that pizza tasted; the waiters coming out with big round platters of pizza held up high. I'm sure the relief of getting all of us there in one piece had something to do with it, but no pizza has ever tasted that good to me.

Uncle Emmet used to take us out driving to see The Morse Chain Works after dark; that was always his favorite thing to do. It looked like a bracelet in the sky. There were lights at the top and at the bottom, and it was straight, like a train and that's all you'd see was those lights, like a rhinestone bracelet.

Joe was about seven, and I allowed him, Michael and James to go out walking as long as they were with Johnny and Bobby. But the older boys had gone all the way out to Cascadilla Gorge, and Joe went after them, thinking he could catch up. When he went missing, I called the police who came over and asked where he went, then fetched Joe and brought him back to me at Snyder's. It happened again the next day. Joe ran off after the older kids and the same guy brought him back. He said "Boy, this kid gets around!"

A few nights later, the boys got out and got inside the Chain Works. The police brought them home and asked, "Do you know where your boys are? Well you might want to keep an eye on them." They stayed pretty good after that.

I was apologetic, but he said, "You know, I don't mind, you call as much as you want, I'll always get him back for you. If it wasn't for Bob Gifford, I wouldn't be where I am today. He was such a mentor to me!" Of course that led into all kinds of talk about Doane's store. I remembered him then, he was a Scaglione boy. I can't remember his first name. He came from a large Italian family. He could have gone one way or another, but ultimately chose the right path, thanks to Giff's influence.

It is so easy for parents to look back and say, "Gee, I wonder if my children will remember the good things we tried to do for them?" Stories like these prove that our efforts are worth it.

Making a Family

Family Portrait, Shippensburg, Pennsylvania May 14, 2016
Johnny, Bobby, Joe, Michael, Camille, John, Janice, and James

JANICE'S FAMILY - HORTONS AND DUNTONS

Barnabas Horton, Long Island

My mother, Doris, was a Horton before she married my father. The first Horton to reach the New World was Barnabas Horton, who came over on a ship in 1640, twenty years after the Mayflower, and founded Southold, Long Island. They were seeking religious freedom in a new country. Before they got off the boat, they had to sign a pact, which was like the first constitution.

They had brought a big rock with them. After Barnabas died, they buried him at the point and used the rock for his memorial. It says "Here lies Barnabas Horton, and though he be dead he speaketh." There may be a plate with a picture of the boat as a memento in our third floor bedroom at the farm house.

The Horton Point Lighthouse was constructed by the U.S. Lighthouse Service in 1857 on the "Cliff Lot" of Barnabas Horton's original 1640 land grant.

Our Cousin Betty who later married a Brady, was George Horton's daughter from his first marriage. I didn't pal with her because she was my sister Jeanette's age. I played with Sergene and Ruthie because they were closer to my age.

My Grandpa George Ingersoll Horton

Grandpa Ingersoll George Horton was a stock broker in the 1920's, and had a house in Union Springs, New York. The Hortons were of means, and had servants who did the laundry and things like that. They had a lot of help raising their seven

147

children. George Horton had been married before but his wife died while birthing his oldest, also named George. George Junior was seven when my grandfather married my grandmother Isabelle (who went by Dell) Casler. Together they had four daughters, Jeanette, and Doris (my mother), (Helen) Louise, and Elizabeth (Ibby).

My Grandpa Horton was one of nine children and a Presbyterian minister. His father, George Dinsmore Horton, was also a very devout Presbyterian, and he had fifteen children.

When we went to visit in the summer, we just enjoyed all of it because they had four girls (our aunts), and we had such fun playing with the cousins. On Sundays, Grandpa Horton was very strict about going to church. Grandma Horton was a Baptist, I believe, and stayed home to take care of the house and prepare the meals. She did the cooking. When I say they had servants, they did the laundry.

Although we brought a lot of play clothes, we made sure to bring a church dress. No slacks in church, you wear your skirts and dresses.

1910 Horton Family - Jeanette, Doris, George, Arthur Louise, Isabelle Jeanette Hites with unknown baby, Elizabeth (Ibby), and George Ingersoll Horton

My Aunt Jeanette

My Aunt Jeanette died in 1957. She was the oldest daughter, older than my mother. She went in for an operation for a blood clot on her brain, and died shortly after the operation. It didn't go well. We were living in Fair Haven, New Jersey when my mother came to visit and told me. Mother was in a shock about her sister's death, because my Aunt Jeanette had felt very well right up until the operation, well enough to do all her cleaning and everything. My mother said that when she got there, the house was immaculate. Both Aphia and Camille look like my Aunt Jeanette.

Jeanette used to complain that her sister Doris (my mother) was always busy, so there was always a mess around. She'd think she had everything cleaned up, and then Doris would be into another project. My mother earned the nickname "Fuss Bucket" by her family because she never stayed still. She was always fussing around with something. Divine unrest is what my grandma called it.

My Mother, Doris Horton

Doris and her sister Ibby

My mother used to tell me how strict her father was. If they were out even a minute past 6:00 p.m., they would be locked out of the house and have to sit out on the steps, no matter how cold it was.

My mother went to a two-year college where she took elocution and theater, in addition to her other classes. It wasn't mandatory; in those days you didn't have to go to school. In school, she won an opportunity to take a screen test, but her father wouldn't let her travel to California. He didn't want her to be a movie star.

Her grandfather, George Dinsmore Horton, would come visit my grandfather when my mother was growing up, and he would always get all seven kids together to pray. My mother would bring something to eat because she would get bored with all the prayer. She never got caught.

George Horton's Letter

George Ingersoll Horton's words to his children when he was 80 years old, on the occasion of his and Grandmother Horton's Fiftieth Wedding Anniversary circa 1945:

H·O·R·T·O·N

"Horton is from the Latin word "Hortus" and means "Garden." Prior to the last 75 or 100 years practically all of our ancestors were tillers of the soil. Since then history says of them, "Soldiers in every conflict, ministers in the churches, educators in schools and colleges, farmers and landowners, physicians, lawyers, judges, magistrates, legislators, mechanics, builders, ship and mill owners, financiers, business men, writers, artists, diplomats - sturdy, independent, industrious, known for piety, probity and law abidingness.

MOTTO
"The motto on the Horton Coat of Arms is "quod vult valde vult" and means, "What he wills he wills cordially (freely) and without stint.

LINEAGE

"Barnabas, Joseph, David, Daniel, Hon. William, James, George, George, George, Irving

"With Irving the Horton line ends. We will have to leave it to our cousins and others to carry on the name. Disappointed? A little. Now grandchildren and children I don't want you to think that I am trying to make you believe the name Horton is better than the name you bear, or any other name for that matter, but I want you to take pride in your own name and be careful not to do anything that would bring that name into bad repute. I have a feeling that I am getting ready to give some advice.

"It is my wish that you all have a good reputation in the community in which you live. Webster says "Reputation is the estimation in which a person is held by others." I want you all to have character, strong character, the quality or qualities which distinguish a person, especially high qualities, moral force.

"You all want to be successful; success is the attainment of anything you may attempt. I expect that at least half of you would say you want money and you would then be a success. If you should find, or someone should give you a large sum of money the chances are a thousand to one that it would not do you any good but plenty of harm. If you should earn it the hard way that would be different. If you acquire it you know the value of it.

"'Success of any kind worth having must carry with it service.' Do more than you are paid for doing. Character is absolutely necessary to success, but service to others is the quickest way to develop character. Remember the Golden Rule. Do justly, love mercy and walk humbly with your God. Your grandfather is a strong believer in the good that comes from regular church attendance.

"Now to sum up the matter; it would seem that service is an important factor. Don't stop with one good turn a day, get in as many as you can. Be the girl or boy that Mother and all the neighbors like to see coming. Be likable; make yourself popular at home and at school. Service will assure you of the best kind of success."

- George Ingersoll Horton

Turkey Hill Duntons

My grandparents on my father's side were Grandpa Samuel and Grandma Matilda Wait Dunton. They were Scottish and lived on a farm with their three children: Frank, Mabel, and Roderick. Samuel died when I was three. I remember him sitting in his over-stuffed chair with the magazine rack and a standing lamp.

There was no plumbing or electricity at the Dunton farm up on Turkey Hill (later renamed Mt. Pleasant), so my father would spend the summer doing things the old-fashioned way. They had no heat, but they did have two big pot-bellied stoves.

My father had a Chevrolet dealership in Elmira and was very proud of his cars. He would insist on driving his car up the old dirt road to his family's farm, but got so angry when he got stuck my sister Jeanette would say, "If you get angry again, I'm not going."

At that time, Grandma Matilda Dunton had moved from the farm and was living with her cousin Maud. Maud was an elderly woman, my grandmother's age, and she was like the matriarch of the family. She didn't like it if anyone smoked or drank in the family. My father didn't like to go there because he did both. Tillie later moved to Mabel's and then she did all the cooking.

My grandmother found it too hard up there alone at the farm. My father used to talk about tunneling through the snow out the back and then climbing up to the top and snowshoeing to school. My Uncle Frank kept the chickens even after the barn collapsed. Frank's son, my cousin Frankie, and I used to have a lot of fun riding on the tractor with his Dad. It was lots of fun staying at the farm in the summer.

Aunt Mabel had a beautiful rose garden up at the farm and was always working in it. The first thing I would do was visit the garden, and even though I resolved not to end up with a thorn in my finger, I always did. Then I'd go into the house and try to hide it from my Uncle Emmet, but he would find me out and dig them out with his knife. I'd protest, but he would tell me, "You've got to obey your Aunt Mabel and not touch them!"

Tillie with her great grandson Brian Gifford

We used to brush our teeth outside on the porch off the kitchen, and we could see all the way down to the lake. There was a path going down to the outhouse. When we stayed there, we had what you called a chamber pot, a big potty with a cover on it, and our grandmother would always remind us, "Don't forget to empty your chamber pot." And the way we did it was take it down to the outhouse and put it into one of the holes.

Monkey Run was a little pond where people would go swimming in the summer. We'd look out the back window and wait until we'd see the dust from the car. It was my Uncle Frank with Aunt Emma and my cousin Frankie, and he'd take us all down to Buttermilk Falls. It seemed like it was a long ride because this was nearly all the way to the top. My uncle would look up to the very top and tell us, "Now, don't go up there; there's bobcats up in there." On the other side was the Cornell game land.

Years later, when we were living on City Island, John drove the five of us to visit Aunt Mabel and Uncle Emmet. He took us all to the lake cottage, and up to the farm where we slept upstairs in sleeping bags. It was nice, us sleeping upstairs with John and our three young children: Camille, Johnny, and Bobby. Camille was four. John was happy, real happy.

At that time, Aunt Mabel had the farm up for sale for $11,000 and there was a real special piano in it that my great Cousin Maud had left to the farm after she died. It was a square piano, built like an organ without pipes, but not high like an upright.

Love at First Sight

My father, Roderick Dhu Dunton, was sixteen when he met my mother, Doris Casler Dunton. She was twenty-one. Roderick was her younger sister Ibby's boyfriend, but Ibby wanted to stand him up. Ibby told Doris, "You just entertain him, he'll be alright." and dashed out the door. My mother was so mad because she had planned to spend the day cleaning the house and now she was going to have to look after this kid.

When he came to the door and she opened it, she looked down for a scrawny boy and realized she was looking at his waist. So she looks up at this 6'4" guy and fell in love with him that very moment. She couldn't believe that he was so handsome and so adult looking, and she never dreamed he'd be that tall. Aunt Ibby didn't date him after that, and there wasn't any friction except he never liked Ibby after that.

Roderick came from a Scotch/Irish family with a farm outside of nearby Ithaca. His family wasn't as well off as my mother's, but they were in love. They were married on January 5th, 1924 in a double wedding with another one of Doris's sisters, Helen Louise and Austin Zimmer. We always referred to Helen Louise as Louise.

My Mother's Stroke

In 1984, when my mother was eighty-four, she had a stroke. It was November 5th and right on the heels of Nana's stroke in mid-October. At the time, my mother was living in Bradenton, Florida with Mrs. Brooks. She took care of her and slept in the same room with her, and did everything for her, including all of her cooking. They had a cleaning woman.

My mother was a nurse's aide. Before moving to Florida, she lived in Romulus, New York, taking care of Dr. Reimer's invalid wife. She lived with them in a nice house by Cayuga Lake. All her jobs were live-in jobs. Before that she lived with Mrs. Day, a widow in Ithaca in a lovely big house next to a stream.

When we lived in Shippensburg, I had this cold that I couldn't get over and Camille and Johnny talked me into going to Mrs. Day's. I just needed a rest and I did get better just relaxing and listening to the stream. My mother used to say, "Let the peepers put you to sleep." Camille and Johnny did a good job of running the house while I was gone.

Doris at Cayuga Lake

I had been down to Florida the year before to help my mother after she had pneumonia. She had lost a lot of weight during her stay in the hospital.

At the time of her stroke, my mother was reading a biography or autobiography about/by Eleanor Roosevelt in the other room, so she wouldn't disturb Mrs. Brooks. She was so interested in the book, she read late into the night.

When my mother heard Mrs. Brooks wake up, she went into her bedroom to help her start her day. First, she sat on the bed for a minute telling Mrs. Brooks all about the book. Then my mother got up and went to the closet for Mrs. Brooks' clothes and, all of a sudden, collapsed.

Mrs. Brooks called my mother's younger sister, Louise Dolan (age eighty-two), who lived in Sarasota, and Louise called an ambulance. There were four sisters; Jeanette, Doris, Louise, and Ibby.

They took my mother to the hospital in Bradenton and she was in ICU. Aunt Louise called my sister, Jeanette, who called me. I had just returned from church where I was organizing a clothing drive, and I told Jeanette as soon as I found someone to take my place, I'd come down. I quickly was able to find someone to take over, and the next morning, John took me down to the bus station and bought a bus ticket to Sarasota for about $200. My cousin, Beverly (Louise's daughter) picked me up and gave me a place to stay in her home in Sarasota, about half an hour away from Bradenton.

I arrived too late to go to the hospital, so Beverly and I got caught up with each other, and watched Masterpiece Theater. The next day when I went to visit my mother, the nurse invited me to feed her. She ate for me, and the nurses were amazed because, for three days, she had not accepted food from them.

I was allowed to stay with my mother in the hospital for eight hours a day, so I did. It was a strain, because she couldn't talk. When I returned to Beverly's, I was in shock. "I just grew up overnight," I told Beverly. "Do you want to keep on?" Beverly asked, and I said, "Oh, of course, of course."

Mrs. Brooks needed someone to stay with her, since my mother was in the hospital, so I went and stayed with her. One of her relatives came in every day to stay with her while I was away visiting my mother in the hospital.

Mrs. Brooks really missed my mother and wanted her back. "Well, she'll get better," Mrs. Brooks said, because my mother always got better. My mother had a strong constitution. Mrs. Brooks was remembering the time she got pneumonia and sprung right back.

At this point, I thought, "I need my family around me!" so I went to stay with my Aunt Louise and Uncle Bob Dolan. Their son Michael, who everyone called Buddy, was also staying there at the time. Buddy invited me to go hang gliding to give me a break. He felt sorry for me because I was spending eight hours a day just sitting with my mother in the hospital. I went with him, but I didn't fly. I was fifty I guess. He also wanted me to go in and chase the bulls. To do something exciting, he said, but I declined.

It meant a world of difference for me to stay with the Dolans. Uncle Bob Dolan was a horseman and so were their two sons, Buddy and Richard, who everyone called Dickie.

Dickie's daughter was real close to her Uncle Bob Dolan, and they often talked on the phone about horses and such. Buddy was a horse whisperer, and I don't think he had any children.

Louise's first husband, Austin Zimmer, died of cancer. He was the father of Beverly and Bobby. Bobby said, "I know you're not supposed to have favorites, but I just love that Dickie."

By now, it had been about two weeks since my mother had the stroke, and she was doing well enough to get out of ICU and into the nursing home. She was learning how to blow out a match, which was part of the therapy for her throat. Her stroke had been massive, and her right side was paralyzed.

I went home for Thanksgiving and returned to find my mother had begun to gain independence. Disobediently so. They would prop a pillow under her arm and come back to see she had thrown it on the ground.

You couldn't ever hold my mother down. She never really got sick, and really believed in mind over matter. She was really good about taking care of herself. One of her staples was baking soda. It was her cure all for a lot of things. When my Tums don't work anymore, I use baking soda, and it works.

The nursing home staff was happy to have me back because it took my mother's mind off her arm, which was still swollen and had very little feeling. They were impressed by her overall physical fitness. "What did she do?" they asked me, "Did she work out? Because she has the agility of a twenty-year-old." I explained that it was her custom to walk two miles a day. Plus she was in the profession of caring for others.

At the nursing home, I would comb my mother's hair and help her in the bathroom. She was beginning to talk again. I helped her wash her hands, and she showed her appreciation by saying in broken words, "Doon't.... knoww.... much.... mean.... me" which meant "You don't know how much you mean to me."

My mother had beautiful hands. She worked with them so much during her life that they were usually red and raw, but here in the nursing home her hands had regained their natural beauty.

Being close to her like that, I knew every little sound she made. The nurses exclaimed, "We can't understand anything she says." It was a great education for me. What my mother had done for me, I was now able to do for her.

We got to the point where decisions needed to be made regarding finances. My mother had stocks and bonds, and I agreed to be her power of attorney. So, I filled out all the necessary forms and brought them to my mother. The nurses had taught her how to write with her left hand, and she was able to sign her name.

After a couple of weeks, I had to come home to Shippensburg to get ready for Christmas. On my last night with my mother, I kept trying to talk to her but she was glued to her TV. Finally, I had to turn it off so I could tell her I was leaving. I was the world's biggest crybaby in the nursing home, but now when I cry, it's because something beautiful has touched me.

My mother thought I had abandoned her, and refused to eat. So I called every day and sent notes. I had her mail forwarded and every night dealt with whatever needed taken care of.

I was trying to think of a way to bring my mother to Shippensburg. One day when I called the nursing home, Mrs. Brooks' relative was visiting and talked with me on the phone. She told me they were doing their best to get her to eat. The next step was going to be a feeding tube.

So I got tough. They gave her the phone and I said, "Mother, you can't decide when you are going to die. Only God can make that decision." She put the phone down, and Aunt Louise picked it up and asked, "What did you say to her? She didn't like what you said to her at all!" I was too upset to continue the conversation and hung up. I ran out to the car and drove over to the church.

I prayed a novena to Saint Therese, the Little Flower. Before I finished the novena, I had this awareness of everyone in the world being moved by God's love, which is his Holy Spirit. And when we decide to commit suicide, we have pulled away from his love.

And suddenly, I had this feeling, so I got back in the car, finishing the novena on the drive home. I ran into the house and called the nursing home. The nurse said, "She's eating right now." I assumed they had given her the feeding tube. "No," she said, "after you left we brought food in for the last time, and she started eating." What a blessing that was!

My mother eventually got out of the hospital and went to stay with Aunt Louise. I planned to go back in the spring. I could just picture her there sitting on Louise's porch and we'd be so happy. I kept telling myself, "You just look forward to that."

My mother was eating again and gaining strength, and they said that she could return home to Aunt Louise's. They trained Buddy to lift her and Aunt Louise to give her a sponge bath. Buddy assured me that she wouldn't be alone, that they would visit her. "Don't you worry at all; she will not be left alone."

But my mother had another stroke and died the 2nd of February. They called the ambulance right away, and she died in the ambulance on the way to the hospital.

Aunt Louise had called my sister, Jeanette and told her. Jeanette called me right away. I thought about the communion of the saints, and how once you die, everything is known, and I said, "You know, it's a wonderful thing to know, now, that she knows how much we all loved her."

For the next six months, I asked the kids to get the mail. I just couldn't bear the absence of my mother's letters. My mother had also left me a beautiful full length camel's hair coat with a warm, brown fur collar and matching hat. As pretty as it was, it took me two years before I could make myself wear it.

JOHN'S FAMILY - ILLOS AND KOMINSKYS

Camille: John's paternal grandmother, Mary Ann Illo, was born in Palermo, Sicily. When she was seven, she and her parents, Giovani and Camille De Francis, and two sisters Marietta and Rosa, sailed to New Orleans, Louisiana U.S.A. They lived on Rampart Street in what is now the Vieux Carre, or French Quarter section of New Orleans. The girls went to Catholic school taught by Sisters of Ursuline and attended mass at St. Louis Cathedral.

1873 John Peter and Mary Ann Illo

Mary Ann married John Peter Illo, a man chosen for her by her father. He was a barber by trade and had also emigrated from Sicily. Their family name, Aiello, was changed to Illo sometime after 1860. John and Mary Ann bought a wagon and team of horses, and took off across the country.

They had nine children; five sons, and four daughters, beginning with Fred. Then came Annie, Camille, Peter, Joseph, Mary (also known as May, and called Mamie by our family), and John. Frank, John's father, was born in Austin, followed by Josephine, in Dallas. There were other births, but these are the children who survived into adulthood.

1887 Mary and John Peter Illo Family - Camille, Peter, Annie holding a baby (can't read the name, but it should be Mary), Joe, and Fred

The 1900 Dallas census shows the Illo family living at 374 Elm Street. Sicily is listed as the place of birth for fifty-eight-year-old John, fifty-year-old Mary Ann, and Mary Ann's father, seventy-seven-year-old Peter DeFranchio. Brother Fred is listed at 122 Caddo Street with his wife Daisie, their three children Lillian, Howard, and John. Also in residence were Daisie's mother Muttie Jones, and her brothers Charley and Robert.

Mary Ann Illo

Mary Ann's daughter, Camille, loved her mother very much and helped run the boarding home. Grandpa was born there. He didn't go to school because it wasn't mandatory. He was fourteen when he joined a carnival going east, and that's how he ended up in New York City.

Mary Ann Illo - Texas, 1920's

Nana came from Warsaw, Poland with her family when she was three years old. I heard that she was smuggled out beneath the hay in a horse-pulled cart, probably so they wouldn't have to get her a visa.

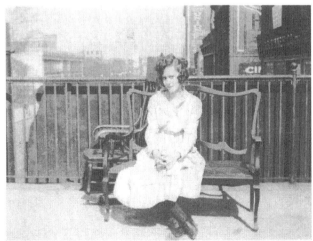

Helen in New York - she went by her stage name Helen Allison

Grandpa Frank Illo met Helen Kominsky (Nana) at the theatre where she was working as a chorus girl. Frank was the house carpenter at the New Burlesque Theater, which is now the Apollo. His commute to work was a three block walk north.

Helen had a nice voice, was light on her feet, and had gotten tired of cleaning houses. So she joined the chorus. After Frank and Helen were married, she'd invite everyone who worked with Frank over, saying, "We'll push back the furniture and dance!" Grandpa always said that Nana brought him good luck. He liked to gamble and had his own room in the basement of the Shubert Theatre in New York, where they played cards.

1918 - Helen and Frank (on the right) with a friend.
Helen is sixteen and pregnant with Frank Jr. She gave birth to Frank in an
apartment building at 257 West 122nd Street, in Harlem.

A Polish Ghetto

As I was looking through the papers on my desk, I came across one of John's articles printed September 16, 2011 in the Shippensburg NEWS-CHRONICLE. It was a rebuttal to someone who wrote that all ghettos were bad. Here's what he wrote:

In Defense of Ghettos

"The word "ghetto" comes from the Italian borghetto, the diminutive of borgo, the word for borough or city, like the German Burg. It means a small borough or city, or a small city within a city.

"Some people, like Jonathan Kozol, writing about the South Bronx in AMAZING GRACE (1996), believe that there are no "good ghettos" - that all ghettos are deplorable because they segregate some people from the general population, and any ghetto, such as Harlem or the South Bronx tends to become impoverished, decayed, given over to drugs and crime. But Kozol is wrong. There are good ghettos. My mother grew up in one.

"When my grandparents brought my mother as a baby here from Poland (then part of Russia) in 1904, they moved into a Polish ghetto in Brooklyn, in a section called Greenpoint, one of the poorest sections of the borough or the city (It's now being gentrified.) The Poles who lived there were poor immigrants, but they were all Poles, not the "dumb Polocks" they were in other parts of the city and the country. To make matters worse they didn't speak English and they were Catholics in a Protestant America at a time when religion meant something. The Poles in Greenpoint spoke the same language, ate the same food, went to the same church (Saint Stanislaw) and sent their children to the same Catholic schools, where they learned English. They did not feel segregated, they were at home.

"And their ghetto was clean and orderly. You've heard of sidewalks so clean you could eat off them. The sidewalks in Greenpoint were that clean, not a gum wrapper or cigarette butt, not a spot of dirt. And despite a nearby elevated railroad, Greenpoint was quiet and orderly. Drugs, crime? Nothing.

"My Grandparents lived in a second-floor walk-up apartment. Their place was surely not opulent, but it was clean, and in the dining room was a large glass-framed picture of Washington and

Kosciuszko and the American and Polish flags. They were all Poles, but they were thankful to be in America.

Helen's mother and brother

"On a small coal stove my grandmother cooked chicken-foot soup - cost her nothing, for chicken feet were thrown away by the butcher, as were bones. And my grandfather and his sons worked - hard. My Uncle Charley worked in two brass foundries and slept at home for half an hour between them. Uncle Al fought in France in the AEF in World War I.

"The ghettos of which Kozol writes are not Polish ghettos, and few of the people work there, other than those who sell drugs. They consume (they're on welfare and food stamps) without producing. Not so the Polish ghetto of Greenpoint. But the liberal Kozol deplores ghettos because they isolate people from the mainstream of the city population, as though that were a vice. To the liberal it is a vice, for he wants everyone to resemble himself, with the same social and political values or neo-values. He extols superficial differences among people - diet, skin color, anatomical details, difference of race (though the liberal won't use that word.)

"But value beliefs are another matter. He would welcome and tries to produce a world of ideological clones. He tolerates religion in others, respecting the "free exercise" clause of the First Amendment, but he'd rather that such obsolete beliefs (to him superstitious) would go away. And he resents little cities within cities - ghettos - where people unlike him can associate and enjoy the freedom to cherish their inherited culture and belief. In Greenpoint my mother's family had that freedom."

John P. Illo - Shippensburg

Nana

Camille: Born in Poland in 1902, Helen Kominsky was fifty-six when I came into the world. She had a fifth grade education and was real proud of her son John for earning a Ph.D. and becoming a college professor.

Helen left home at fifteen and went to work for an Irish family who treated her badly. She wasn't a big fan of the Irish after that, but both sons married women with Irish blood. I imagine she was a difficult mother-in-law.

As the first of her eight grandchildren and the only girl, I earned a special place by her side, often spending the weekends at her home in Atlantic Highlands, New Jersey. Nana would push me around the house in a wheeled laundry cart as she went about her chores.

Nana was active in her garden club and the Democratic Party, and enjoyed the company of dogs. Before I could walk she would put me on a blanket on her beautiful lawn and ask her black lab, Sissy, to keep an eye on me. She was fond of the name Susi and generally had a dog with that name. When one Susi died, she'd name the next new dog Susi.

Nana Helen had a giant picture window built into the living room so she could watch the birds in her rose garden. Her yard was beautifully landscaped with mature trees, all manner of blooming shrubs, and a play garden for her grandchildren, framed in lawn-capped rock walls. Her son, Frank, and his wife, Kathy (my uncle and aunt) lived next door with her grandsons, Frank and Mark. have many fond memories of weekends at Nana's with my brothers and cousins. The extended family often joined us all for Sunday dinner.

Nana and Susi

Grandpa Frank's brother, Jody, Helen Frank, and Jody's wife, Mabel

Nana had a vegetable garden with a hot house, and was a superbly gifted cook. Her son, my Uncle Frank, often remarked that his mother could take two stones, rub them together, and produce the most delicious soup he'd ever tasted. Summer Sundays featured fried chicken, potato salad, corn on the cob, sweetened ice tea, and cake or pies underneath the violet leaves of an enormous plum tree.

No one has been able to reproduce her chocolate chip cookies, even though I watched her bake them many times. She started with dairy butter from a doe-eyed Jersey cow, but only on a day with the right combination of temperature and humidity. In winter, she stepped outside with her cookie sheet and waved it in the cold air before loading it up again.

Nana was a dancer on the chorus line. She used her stage name, Helen Allison, on her marriage certificate to hide the fact that she was Polish. She was proud of her arms, and it pained her to watch her hands cripple and swell with arthritis as she aged. She was always up before anyone else in the house.

Sunday dinner at Nana and Grandpa's
Grandpa, at the head of the table at the bottom of the photo, Nana to his
right, with Nicky and Irene on the other end of the table. It's likely either
Stevie or John climbed onto the bedroom roof for this shot

When my father was growing up, he had asthma, so Nana would get up early and dust the house before he got out of bed in the morning.

Helen and Frank lost their second child, a little girl named Rita, when she was five months old. To the day. Rita was born April 8, 1923 and died on September 8 of "congenital malformation of bile ducts." Nana gave her name as Helen Allison on the death certificate.

Rita's death threw Nana into a tailspin, and earned her a couple of appointments with the electro shock machine. She blamed herself for Rita's death, and fell into a depression, telling my mother many years later, that she had caused her baby's death by "neglect". She received therapy and medication (lithium, etc. - what she called "nerve pills") all of her life.

Nana told me she decided to end her life at one point, but when she went downstairs, she found a litter of newborn puppies. Unable to leave those little dogs to fend for themselves, she changed her mind. It was my good fortune that Nana decided to stick around.

The Orphans

Nana always referred to the Wallace kids as the orphans. She was fifteen when her parents took "Little" Helen, Irene and Stevie Wallace in as babies because their parents died. We don't know the circumstances of their death. Their mother was Nana's aunt. Her married name was Lipske, so it's unclear where they got the name Wallace. The third sister (Nana's other aunt) was Jane Haruki Greguski. Nana's mother's name was Kominsky. Haruki, Lipske, and Kominsky.

Nana didn't think the family should be taking in three more kids when they already had five, so she left home to work for an Irish family. Two years later, she was married to Frank Illo and giving birth to her own first child, Frankie.

When Nana's parents could no longer take care of the orphans, Nana and Grandpa took them in. By now, Irene was eleven, and Nana and Grandpa had two sons, Frank and John. Nana put Irene in charge of John, who was six years younger than Frank.

When Nana was thirty, she and Grandpa went to Europe on an ocean liner and left Irene in charge. Irene would have been eighteen, and Frank and John who would have been thirteen and seven.

I always admired Grandpa, especially because he wasn't a blood relative to the Wallace kids, but he adored them as if they were his own. He couldn't talk enough about Helen Wallace or "Little Helen" as she was referred to so she wouldn't be confused with Nana Helen.

Little Helen worked with Grandpa in the rag shop on Broadway in New York. That's where all the old costumes were returned and made into new costumes. Little Helen was the seamstress. Grandpa Frank and Little Helen just loved each other and she loved her work in the Rag Shop.

Helen Verges with photos of Pope Paul II and Joseph Illo

Marguerite Jarvis (her father, Calvin Jarvis married grandpa Frank's sister, Mary) was raised in Texas. That was her home place. She and Little Helen introduced each other to their husbands. Little Helen introduced Marguerite to Tom Lyons of Highlands, New Jersey, and Marguerite introduced Little Helen to Jim Verges from Texas.

Little Helen married Jim in Texas and they had two sons. Marguerite married Tom and had four or five children. One of her daughters was so pale she looked like an albino but she turned out to be the prettiest of the bunch.

Janice and John, laughing with the photographer, Stevie Wallace, on their wedding day

Stevie became a professional photographer and was a gag-a-minute kind of guy. One time Nana walked in wearing a brocade dress, and Stevie cried, "Bridget!" in a French accent, drink in hand. Stevie and John were cut-ups together, and he took our wedding photos.

Irene was so small-she was under 5 feet tall. Nana was 5'2." Irene's feet were so small that she could always get a bargain on very expensive shoes. They sold the shoes they had used in the window displays at reduced prices because they were a little faded from being in the window.

The doctor said Irene's pelvis never matured beyond that of a ten-year-old girl and advised her not to have children. But Irene married Nicky Egidio and survived the birth of their two daughters, Barbara and Linda. Again, Grandpa loved them just like they were his own. They would often find their way onto his lap. Barbara's last name is Holstein now. Holstein, just like the cow. Linda's first marriage didn't work out.

Barbara had a screw in her shoulder because she had broken it. When she complained about the pain, John said, "Well, of course it hurts with that screw in there!" She didn't realize the hardware went all the way through and was embarrassed.

Nicky came from a large family. After I married John, Nicky used to sing "Lucky lucky lucky me," carrying the latest baby, singing and showing them off.

Nana was president of the Democratic Society, but when her term was up, they didn't vote her back in as president. Not wanting to show any ill will, she offered to take everyone out to dinner at the restaurant where Nicky was working as a chef and I went, too.

Grandpa Frank Illo

Camille: My grandfather was a happy guy who lived in "The City" and came down to Jersey on the weekends. Nana would pick him up at the bus station in her Studebaker. He was hard of hearing and loved baseball. On Sundays when the whole family gathered on the lawn with drinks, kids adventuring in the woods, dogs panting behind them, Grandpa would be sitting in the middle of the hubbub sprawled in a lawn chair with his huge radio held up against his ear.

Grandpa was fourteen when he joined the carnival and came east from Texas. He wanted to be in show business. You didn't have to go to school in those days. They just helped their parents on the farm because they were needed.

Grandpa was head carpenter of eleven theaters in New York City owned by the Shubert brothers. The main one was called the Shubert Theater, and the other ten had different names. I think there were three Haruki brothers who all worked with Grandpa. Grandpa invented the color wheel in

1940, a wheel you would put on a stage light to create different colored light.

Camille: According to Popular Science magazine's September 1919 issue, Frank Illo also invented a sound effects machine involving cylinders, shafts, steel drums, bells, and compressed air tanks.

Grandpa Frank with his sister, Mamie. Camille is second from the right.

Grandpa died a month short of his ninetieth birthday in 1976. About ten years later I was talking with Frank Haruki and his wife on the phone. Mr. Haruki told me how he loved Frank Illo and how he was where he was today because of him. "I owe him everything," he said. His wife (I think her name was Mary) was principal of a Catholic school. The Haruki boys used to stay with Nana in the summers, just like Tommy did.

Nana and Marguerite, Johnny, and Janice, pregnant with Bobby

Nana Helen and Grandpa Frank with Camille and Johnny - 1958

I didn't know Grandpa couldn't read and write until we were out at Nana's one day, and he kept asking John to look up this or that. I asked John, "Why is he asking you to do this?" "Don't you know?" John replied, "My father never learned to read or write." This explained why Little Helen was such a big help to him. She had gone to school through the fifth grade and learned to read and write.

A Winter in Connecticut

Nana wanted to leave her home in New Jersey, so she went to Connecticut for a while. She and Grandpa were having a hard time paying for both the house in Jersey and his apartment in Manhattan and it was coming time for him to retire, so she was thinking of selling the house.

Grandpa told me he wanted to come home to raise white pigeons, but Nana was so used to living alone that she wanted him to stay in New York. There wasn't any one thing about him. She was just used to her freedom, and since he didn't drive, she would have to be his driver.

He lived at The Whitby at 325 45th Street in Hell's Kitchen and came down to Jersey on the bus for the weekends. He never really lived at Nana's, but he had a small bedroom across from the bathroom. He went there on the weekends, returning to New York on the bus Sunday night. Grandpa would talk with me about pets. He said his mother had a cat and a boarding house. I think there were eight kids in his family.

It became a feud between them. Nana had gotten really angry with grandpa when he inherited about ten thousand dollars from his brother, Jody, and gave some of it to his niece Marguerite Lyons. Marguerite had five daughters and her oldest daughter, Camille, wanted to go to college but she couldn't afford it.

Nana and John were talking in the kitchen, and I heard her say she couldn't afford two places now that Grandpa was retired. So she rented out her house and either rented or house sat a house in Connecticut. She took Camille, Johnny, and her neighbor, Lee Baines, who was about Johnny's age up to Connecticut. It wasn't long before she got homesick and moved back.

Nana brought me back a blue vase. It was so pretty. She said, "If you have something you want to grow, you put it in there and it'll sprout." So I did, and it worked. The plant sent out little roots that looked like bean threads.

Camille: I remember the road trip north. It was a cold, bright, sunny day when we all stopped at a roadside tourist trap. It was me, Johnny, and Lee, Nana and another woman, one of her friends. Nana bought long matches to use to start the fire in the fireplace in Connecticut. I'd never seen matches that size and was quite taken by them.

Up at the house, it was snowing like crazy. I recall listening to Crimson and Clover (over and over) on the radio at the Connecticut home. That song came out in late 1968 and was top of the charts in 1968 and 1969 so that must have been the year Nana went to Connecticut. Grandpa would have been eighty-two. When I hear that song today, I am transported to the house in Connecticut with the snow drifts, Lee, and Johnny.

Nana in the Nursing Home

Camille: My Aunt Kathy and Uncle Frank kept an eye on Nana as she aged. Kathy managed her finances and would occasionally find the stove on when she went next door to check on her mother-in-law. Finally, they were faced with the task of moving Nana to a safer place.

After Nana went into the nursing home, she didn't talk much and often did not recognize her family. But sometimes she surprised us.

One time, Nicky and Irene went to visit Nana with a newly-baked cake. Irene went out to get the cake and Nicky, Nana, and I were sitting there talking about missing Nicky and Irene's Rum Runner Restaurant (they had sold the business

179

and retired.) Nana said, "Oh, you'll miss it." Irene returned with the cake and we all sat, and ate, and talked. Nana said, "This is delicious!" It made Frank feel better to know his mother was still able to carry on a conversation.

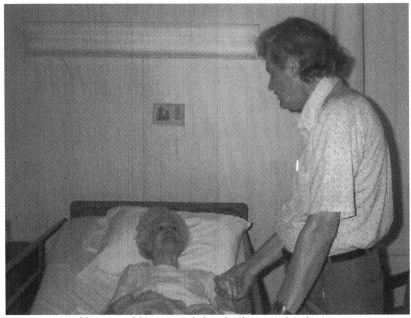

Nana and her son, John, in the nursing home

"She loves me, now; why didn't she love me before?" Irene said. Back when she and Nicky were managing two restaurants, they needed kitchen help, and Nana wanted a job so they hired her. They needed somebody who would take direction and, sadly, it wasn't Nana. Nana would cut away all but the best parts of a vegetable, which was fine for her own kitchen. but too expensive in a restaurant. Irene said, "I can't tell her to push a broom, and clean up like somebody else I'd hire." It was kind of a falling out there.

We remembered how one time Tommy came to visit, and they went to their Colony Restaurant, and Nicky got Tommy a jacket because he was underdressed. There wasn't any dress code at their Rum Runner restaurant in Sea Bright. People could come right in off the beach.

The other day, I had a real nice phone talk with Michael. He said he was interviewing somebody, and he realized he had a talent for that. And said, "Oh, yes!" and told him about a time when we went to visit Nana in the nursing home, and I had gone out to the car for a can of black olives because Nana had expressed an interest in them.

While I was gone, the tape recorder was running. I always taped our conversations. When I played back the tape where Michael was talking with Nana, she just sounded so good with it. She was responding to him and he to her. It was beautiful.

During another nursing home visit, Nana kept telling John, "You look like my son," while he was helping her up and so on, and then she took a good look and said, "You are my son!" and John said, "Yes, that's me, that's me..." And you could hear the tears of joy in his voice. I love listening to this recording.

Nana died June 2nd, 1989 and we all went to New Jersey for her funeral. The night before her funeral, we wanted to bake something special, something she used to make that we all loved, to commemorate her life. Mark had Nana's incredible poppy seed bread recipe, but couldn't figure out how to make it. So together he and I baked a loaf and everyone said it tasted just like Nana's.

After the funeral, I took Joe to see Nana's sister, Sophie, and her husband, Tom Russell in New York. We also went to see Irene and Nicky and meet up with Jane Haruki, the oldest of the Haruki children. Jane had married Tom Greguski, and so we went over to the Greguskis. Bobby was working on a paper, and couldn't get away and he's always regretted it. Finally, we went over to City Island to visit our old neighbors, the Sheridans, the Gouldians, etc.

Tom and Sophie Russell, Joe

Camille: After Nana died, her grandson, Mark, bought her house. Not only did he keep it in the family, but he left it virtually unchanged, turning it into a shrine to Illo family history. He moved a baby grand piano into the living room, topped it with framed family photos, and filled the walls with photos.

Nana's old bedroom, frozen in time

Frank and Kathy

When my sister-in-law, Kathy, gave up smoking, she didn't want to gain weight so she joined Weight Watchers and they refused her. She told Frank, "I'll bet you're the only man with a wife who was rejected by Weight Watchers!"

Kathy Hugart married Frank Illo, Jr. in February, 1959 at Saint Patrick's Cathedral in New York City when Kathy was thirty-two and Frank was thirty-eight.

It was a morning wedding. Frank's little brother, John, was parking the car after driving Nana and I up to New York. She and I started down the aisle towards the main altar, noticing that another wedding ceremony was just finishing up in the left side sanctuary where Frank and Kathy would soon be married.

Kathy and Frank on their Wedding Day

Marine Captain Frank Illo

When John came in, he went directly into the sacristy to prepare for the ceremony. He was going to be the best man, just as Frank had been best man at our wedding.

I had never been to a full Catholic wedding before, and it was beautiful. Just six years before, when we were married, we were married at the altar rail because I was not yet a Catholic.

Nana and I sat in the pews in the front behind Irene and Nicky Egidio with their daughters Barbara and Linda.

Irene was so beautiful! She said, "I'll hold the baby and then you can enjoy it more. Do you mind?" And I didn't mind, so she held Bobby.

Aunt Kathy wore a very attractive suit. It was gorgeous. She was regal and modest. She didn't paint her nails. A lot of people painted their nails in those days, but neither Kathy nor I did.

Frank was always so handsome and charming that the women at the theatre flocked around him, but he didn't pay any attention to them. He was waiting for the love of his life, which turned out to be Kathy.

After the wedding, we were invited to the first reception. There were two receptions that day. The first reception was a small one that Kathy and Frank wanted to have before they got on the ship to Rome for their honeymoon.

So John and I, Nana, Grandpa, Kathy's parents Mr. and Mrs. Hugart and her older sister June, June's husband, and some of Grandpa's family (Marguerite Lyons) took a limousine to the Waldorf Astoria Hotel to celebrate with Frank and Kathy before they headed off to Rome on an ocean liner for their honeymoon. It was "adults only" so Irene kept Bobby and brought him to the second reception with the rest of Nana's family.

While we were at the Waldorf, I had a wonderful conversation with June about why I converted to Catholicism. Her father, Mr. Hugart, gave the toast saying how difficult this day was for him because he was so close to his daughter, yet he was very happy for Kathy.

Mr. Hugart used to treat Kathy and her friends to lunch because he was such a people person. Kathy played the piano and her father liked for her to play "Londonderry Air," and "I'll Take You Home Again Kathleen." "Danny Boy" was a popular version of this 1894 tune.

When we were leaving the reception, Nana kissed Frank and Kathy on their cheeks, and so I followed suit. Frank looked surprised and said, "My sister!", and I felt so happy because I really did feel like a sister to Frank and Kathy.

After the first reception, we drove to Sophie and Tom Russell's in New Hyde Park on Long Island for the second reception. Tom and Sophie had been working hard to finish the family room in time for this reception, and it was lovely with a bar and everything.

Baby Bobby never cried at all. They just passed him around and everyone took turns holding him. I had already weaned him, so he only had to be fed a bottle, and was easy to care for. So I just had the day off with plenty of time to mill around, and it was wonderful talking to everyone.

There was so much family there, mostly from Nana's side because most of Grandpa's family was in Texas. All of Nana's mother's family (the Kominsky's, Lipskis, and Haruki's) were there.

Nana's brother Alfred, whom we all called Al, and his wife, Ann, were there along with her nephew, Billy. Charlie, one of Nana's other brothers, and his daughter, Charlene, were there, too. Charlene had held up my train at my wedding. It was nice to see Nana and Charlie sitting in the foyer talking about their dogs. People were coming in the door, and everyone looked happy.

And that was it! Camille and Johnny stayed overnight at the Duffy's next door to our house on City Island. When we got back, Camille had had a great time and Johnny was in the front yard waiting for us to come home. I think he missed us.

Camille: There were already three of us when Aunt Kathy and Uncle Frank had their first child. Frankie was born the year after Bobby, followed by Mark the year after Joe. We kids all played together and were real close. I found it interesting that both my parents came from two-child families, and that Aunt Jeanette had two children, and Uncle Frank had two as well. My parents were the ones to break the mold and go for six.

1969, Joe's First Communion Standing: Aunt Kathy, Johnny, Joe, Cousin Frank, Bobby, and Cousin Mark. Sitting in the rickshaw James, and Michael

Kathy's Memorial Service January 17, 2014

I was afraid I would be unable to stay in Kathy's house because of my back. But it turned out I was able to get up the front steps, so I cancelled my reservation at the Comfort Inn. Mark and Frank brought a bed down from upstairs, and it was perfect.

Johnny, Bobby, Joe, and James went out to explore their old haunts in the neighborhood and when they got back they said, "Gee, it feels like Aunt Kathy is still here with you in the kitchen." While they were out, the neighbor from across the street, John Alonzo, came by and I mistook him for his son because he looked so young. "Oh, Johnny! You're all grown up!" Turned out he wasn't the son, it was eighty-six-year-old John Alonzo Sr.! I've got wonderful pictures of him and his wife that Johnny took.

Our very own Father Joseph said Kathy's memorial mass at Saint Agnes, Kathy's church. I was one of the readers. Aunt Kathy's ninety-five-year-old sister June, was there with one of her daughters.

John's Family

It was great to see June. She and I really hit it off back when I was new to the family. She read the prayers of the faithful, and I read the first reading. June was the beautiful matron of honor at Kathy and Frank's wedding, and she was still beautiful. I recognized her face instantly. Her two daughters grew up and moved to Boulder, Colorado.

It was so good, looking out across the church and seeing so many people from the past. Three of Marguerite Lyons' daughters were there. It was so fun talking to these three girls.

We all went to dinner at Bahr's, one of Frank and Kathy's favorite restaurants. What a great time filling in all these memories of Grandpa and Nana. The waiter came by for our order about five times, but we were too busy telling family stories to look at our menus. Houston was just agog to hear all these things about her family. And then she'd ask questions! It was so wonderful to be with Joe, Mark, Frankie, and Houston.

Frank and Kathy both had their ashes scattered in the ocean. John said, "But there's no marker! It's just like they never lived." I want to be buried in the ground, whole and intact.

SHIPPENSBURG, PENNSYLVANIA

In 1970, we moved to Pennsylvania from New Jersey because John got a job teaching at Shippensburg State Teacher's College. We paid $14,000 for a house on Orange Street in town, and in July of 1974, we bought the farmhouse on Mud Level Road, about six miles out of town, for $10,400. We hadn't yet sold the house in West Long Branch, so for a time we owned three homes.

The farm house on Mud Level Road

The house on Mud Level Road had been built in 1900 and was showing its age, so we put $7,000 into additions and repairs. For example, the house only had one electrical outlet in each room, so we added two more in each room, as well as washer and dryer hookups, and electric heat. We had to put in new floors because one side was four inches higher than the other!

Mr. Mitten turned the attic into a master bedroom and bath, and sixteen-year-old Bobby showed his engineering talents by installing cabinets and a hallway upstairs. Before that the upstairs rooms were adjoining, one lead to the other, and so even though it made the rooms a little smaller, he moved the walls and made a hallway.

The house was white with green shutters, and Joe had the idea of painting it. I told him how much I loved Jeanette's house with the red shutters, and he said "I can paint them red," because the green was nearly all washed off. So, the whole family got to work and painted them red.

I loved the house for all its big windows and a window over the sink. I always faced east when I'd get down on my knees for morning prayers at the farm. You don't have to be a Catholic to do that. The sun used to pour in from the east and light up the dining room table.

What I loved about that old farmhouse is that the windows went almost from ceiling to floor. When the sun comes in the windows, it gets so warm in Joe's room. When Kathryn and James came up to visit me up in the farm she said, "Oh, this is a snuggly room, I love this room."

Joe's old room became my room, and when I left, it became John's room in the winter. The first time Camille came to the farm with Nana, she and Nana slept in Michael's room. They had hoped to bring Helen Verges but that didn't happen.

~*~

The renters in the house on Orange Street were on welfare and were having trouble paying rent. They had some pretty expensive gifts around and John said, "There's no reason they can't pay the rent." Eventually, we sold that house to a couple who redid the floors beautifully before they moved in.

The boys cultivated their interest in astronomy after receiving a telescope. Michael's interest began in West Long

Branch with an issue of National Geographic Magazine which had two panoramic foldout sections, one showing the ocean floor and the other our galaxy, the Milky Way.

You should have seen this trip that we went on. I mean, driving over to New Jersey from Pennsylvania and back with my three sons. I pulled down the rear view mirror and looked at them in the back seat. "What on earth are you doing there?! I'm not going another inch until you boys settle down."

~*~

I was taking the Three Musketeers, Joe, Mike, and James, to the swimming pool at Shippensburg College in my black, 1968 Volkswagen Beetle, and got stopped by campus police for going fifteen miles over the speed limit. Thereafter, all three called campus security "mommy catchers".

~*~

In Shippensburg, I used to go into the prisons with my Shippensburg Civic Club committee as part of this federated women's project called "Wit to Win" which was working with the National Council on Crime and Delinquency. They would draw up papers for us and the prison board would authorize us to go right into the prisons. They trusted us to go whenever we wanted because we were the wives of men with good reputations.

We went to the school board meetings and interviewed the superintendents in Carlisle, Shippensburg, and the Scotland School for Veterans' Children. There were a lot of kids from the Philadelphia ghettos who came to that school. It was wonderfully fascinating. I even wanted to go up to the college and take a course. We interviewed the judge Chauncey Depew. I realized this was something I liked to do and had a talent for. Once I left my pocketbook at the police station and the police chief called me at home!

~*~

The first and only place I've ever heard a whippoorwill was at Nana's, while crows remind me of our farm on Mud Level Road. Our neighbors, the Kings, had a pet crow that

191

would fly down and sit on my shoulder. The cardinals took a liking to my car, and woodpeckers were pecking at the house before it was re-sided.

My mother came to Shippensburg to celebrate the birth of Johnny and Darla's first child, Aphia, in 1978. The event drew four generations of women; my mother, John's mother, me and Camille, and little Aphia. Nana was showing us how to eat these chips with her tongue reaching for the chip in the palm of her hand.

Three Generations of chip eaters: Helen, Janice, Camille, and Doris

Nana came out again in the early 80's and the house was full, so she and Camille stayed in the University Lodge. That was the time we took pictures of Johnny and Darla's daughters, Aphia and Charity. Charity was already walking.

Aphia visited me in my apartment in town the other day, and when she walked in, she said the smell of what I was cooking reminded her of the farm. The farm was her haven. Johnny and Darla moved to Shippensburg from Rochester when Aphia was fourteen and she was miserable because everyone made fun of her clothes and her New York accent.

The Miracle Girl

The accident happened at 4:20 p.m. on January 5, 2007 but it wasn't dark yet. John and I were on our way to meet Johnny and Darla for dinner. I remember getting ready to go. John was saying, "C'mon we're gonna be late, we won't be able to get a seat in there." I always wanted to look nice for John when I went out with him, so I took a little extra time to put lipstick on, which I wasn't used to doing.

I remember walking towards the car down our sidewalk, but I don't remember getting into the car or anything after that until I was in the ER in York.

I later met the man who plowed into us. He introduced me to his wife. Neither of us could see each other's car lights. I came to a full stop, which I always did. There was a real deep fog where you can't see anything. This happened out there in the country sometimes, a dense fog that settled in the low spots. I remember sometimes having to get out of the car to be able to see. I'd just walk ahead of it with the lights on to see, but that's not what I did this time.

I did stop at the stop sign, and I guess I waited a considerable time, and I couldn't see any lights at the top of the hill to my left. But the other driver wasn't going over the speed limit or anything. And when he was up on the hill, I'm sure there wasn't as much fog up there but that didn't help him see what was down below.

When I pulled into the intersection, we were hit with the full force of his car plowing into my side of the car. I heard that I was pinned between the door and the console, strapped into place with my seat belt. John was able to get out and walk away. He hadn't been wearing a seat belt and his side of the car wasn't hit. He didn't realize he'd jumped out of the car until after he got to the hospital, when he looked down and saw mud on his shoes. We were both taken to the emergency room in ambulances.

Janice's car after the accident

I had a broken neck, leg, ribs, pelvis, and a busted spleen. Months later, Debbee told me that my spleen was punctured by my own ribs, and I found this amazing.

So many people thought I would die after I was pinned in my car that my friends at Our Lady of Visitation nicknamed me, "The Miracle Girl." When the man who served as my speech therapist saw me at Corpus Christi Church in Chambersburg (he was the organist) he didn't recognize me at first. But then he said "You are that woman!", and told me that the hospital ran out of my type of blood in their blood bank, so people were donating blood. Both pastors were ready to give me my Last Rites.

When I was in ICU, the nurses offered to let Bobby's son, Taylor, help move me. But I said, "Honey, they've had training and you haven't." But it was hospital staff that bumped my ankle moving me, creating a sore that took all of a hundred days to heal.

Maybe it was another nurse, but this woman was allowed to pick me up, and she said she could do it alright, but she caught my foot on the railing. And that sore was so bad that, when I went to Shippensburg Health Care Center for rehabilitation, they had to treat it every morning, and every night. It's still tender.

Camille: The Accident threw us all for a loop. Dad walked away from the car, but Mom was pinned between the caved-in door and the console. John, Darla, and James met them at the hospital where the doctor asked them what they wanted to do. "Pull out all the stops," they decided and hospital staff went to work to bring Mom back from the brink of death.

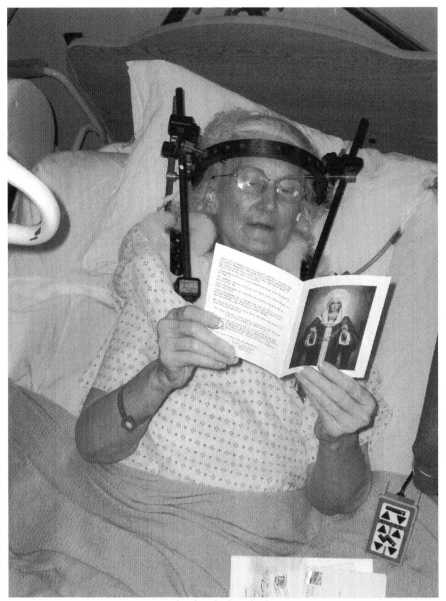

Janice in her halo

April, 2007 - Janice released from the nursing home

Three months later Mom was released from Shippensburg Health Care Center with a neck brace and a cane. We all had doubts that she would ever walk again, but the physical therapists at SHCC did a fantastic job. Mom had beaten the odds, and was back on her feet. Only once did I see her lose heart during her stay in the nursing home. I'd said something about going home and she replied, "This is my home, now."

Sonny and Dolora Mitten

Camille: Johnny's father-in-law, Sonny Mitten, died in 2013. Darla's mother, Dolora, survived him. The Mittens were part of our life for many years because Johnny started dating Darla when she was only sixteen. Sonny had a couple of horses. He loved horses like I do, and was happy to share. So I rode his appaloosa stallion Sonny Boy all over Shippensburg for a year or so while I lived there.

Dolora had a vivacity about her, laughed easily, and was as generous and giving a woman as I've ever met. She was an artist and painted pictures, designs, and words on everything. She even painted Johnny and Darla's children's names on the stair risers in the stone house. She and Sonny were wonderful grandparents to Johnny and Darla's three kids, Aphia, Charity, and Brandon.

Sonny helped build a stone house with his father, and Johnny and Darla later had it moved to Red Oak Lane, a stone's throw from the fairgrounds. Darla was very close to both her parents, and all three traditionally worked the midsummer Shippensburg Community Fair.

On the day of Sonny Mitten's funeral, they picked me up and drove me to the Nazarene Church. I sat behind Aphia and Dolora. It was interesting to hear all the eulogies, and I was surprised to hear that Sonny was a bit wild, running stop signs because he didn't think they were necessary. Dolora sat in the back of the van in her lawn chair. She just snickered, you know, and it put everybody in a good mood.

The main thing that came out was that he had so much love. We didn't do too much crying because of the stories.

Darla had to do all the work that year at the fair because her mother wasn't up to it at eighty-nine! Darla said her father's car was up for sale and parked at the fairgrounds in the same place he always parked. She found this very disturbing, a reminder of his recent death. After a few days though, Darla was able to look at the car and get a different feeling about it. Seeing his car there made her feel that her father really was there instead of gone.

Johnny and Darla's stone house

Sonny Mitten was buried in a simple pine box made by the Mennonites. Simple yet sturdy enough for the pall bearers to carry it.

Family Reunion 2009 - Johnny and Darla's back yard
Standing: Brandon and Joanna with twins Jacob and Bethany, Michael and
Aphia, Bob and Camille, Charity and Jason with Lydia and Alana
Middle Row: Sonny, Dolora, Janice, John
Front Row: Johnny, Darla, Ben, Micah, and Levi

GRANDCHILDREN

Camille: Camille married Bob Armantrout and became stepmother to Emily, Amy, and Molly. Johnny married Darla Mitten, and they had Aphia, Charity, and Brandon. Bobby married Deb Silvis, inheriting Jason and Dara. Together, they had Taylor and Theresa. Joe followed his vocation into the priesthood and presides over a flock of "children" as Father Joseph of Saint Mary Star of the Sea in San Francisco. Michael had a little girl, Nichole. James married Kathryn Winterle, inheriting Christina.

Charity with her father and grandfather at the farm - 1996

Christina married Lou Awad in May of 2012. Come to find out, his family is from Bergen County, and he knows of all these places that we knew! He said Holy Name Hospital was still there, the hospital where I had my first two babies.

Aphia

Aphia is just like Camille. She's like a replay. She hit it off with Nana when she was here, just like Camille did, and I thought, "It's Camille all over again." She looked more like Camille than any of the other kids.

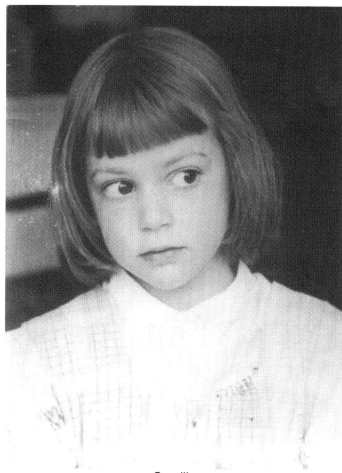

Camille

It was interesting to see what each grandchild was drawn to because each one is so different. What an amazing beautiful gift a human being is. Charity was drawn immediately to the mechanical things. Aphia was drawn to the pottery and this chest of old dated clothes from the 1900s. She liked putting them on. Brandon was pretty little, about four, and would just follow them around, seeing what his older sisters were up to.

Darla loves Man's creative beauty, like 17th century or 18th century pottery. Aphia kind of gets that from her. I used to take Aphia, Charity, and Brandon to the touch me museum down at the library when Darla was going back to school for her med tech degree.

I remember one winter Darla, James, Aphia and I went down to BWI to spend the night so we could catch an early flight. Aphia had an interest in old comedies and things like that, Jack Benny or whatever. James said, "I don't know why but they don't seem funny at all to me." Aphia did a lot of reading, so she had some idea of who these people were. Amos and Andy, you can listen to that any time because they poke fun at themselves rather than famous people of their time.

Taylor with his grandpa and Camille at Bobby and Deb's in Lancaster-1996

CHRONOLOGY

1600 - Barnabas Horton born in Leicester, England
1640 - Barnabas Horton settles in Southold, Long Island
1680 - Barnabas Horton deceased July 13
1862 - Birth George Ingersoll Horton September 24
1871 - Birth Isabelle Jeanette Hites November 5
1886 - Birth Frank Illo, Sr. March 9, Austin, Texas
1898 - Birth Frank Dunton
1900 - Birth Doris Casler Horton January 16
1902 - Birth Helen Kominsky December 15
1905 - Birth Roderick Dhu Dunton
1908 - Birth Mabel Dunton
1914 - Birth Irene Wallace April 18
1919 - Marriage Frank Illo and Helen Allison May 24 Toledo, Ohio
1919 - Birth Frank Illo, Jr.
1923 - Birth Rita Illo April 8
1923 - Rita Illo deceased September 8
1924 - Marriage Roderick Dunton and Doris Casler Horton January 5, Ithaca, New York
1924 - Marriage Austin Zimmer and Helen Louise Horton January 5 Ithaca, New York
1926 - Birth Jeanette Dunton, January 18
1926 - Birth John Peter Illo, April 10
1926 - Birth Kathy (Kathleen) Hugart, May 19
1932 - Birth Janice Louise Dunton, Elmira July 20
1937 - The Great Depression bankrupts the Dunton family
1944 - Move to Ithaca to live with Mabel and Emmet Doane
1945 - Roderick Dhu Dunton deceased October 11
1947 - George Ingersoll Horton deceased February 14
1948 - Marriage Jeanette and Bob Gifford October
1949 - Birth Brian Gifford October 12
1951 - Birth Barbara (Grace) Gifford December 19

Chronology

1953 - Marriage John Peter Illo and Janice Louise Dunton
     July 26 New York, New York

1953-1955 - Bergenfield - Foster Village garden apartments

1954 - Birth Camille Illo June 4

1955 - 1956 - Bergenfield, first home

1955 - Birth Johnny Illo September 7

1956 to 1957 - Norvelt "barn house" rental

1957-1958 - Fair Haven just off of Fair Haven Road

1958-1963 - 393 City Island Avenue, Bronx, New York rental

1958 - Birth Bobby Illo September 16

1959 - Birth (Nephew) Frank Illo November 14

1961- Birth Joe Illo December 4

1962 - Birth (Nephew) Mark Illo August 11

1963-1964 - Avon-by-the-Sea rental

1963 - Birth Michael Illo November 27

1963 - Isabelle Jeanette Hites deceased March 29

1964 -1970 - 64 Hollywood Avenue, West Long Branch

1965 - Birth James Illo July 11

1969 - John Illo gets his Ph.D. from Columbia

1970-1965 - 210 East Orange Street in Shippensburg, PA

1976 - Frank Illo deceased February 1

1985 - Doris Dunton deceased February 2

1986 - John Illo retires from teaching at Shippensburg State
     Teacher's College

1989 - Helen Illo deceased June 2

1993 - Frank L. Illo deceased July 5

1995 - Irene Wallace Egidio deceased December 1

1998 - Bob Gifford deceased February 8

2013 - Kathy (Kathleen) Hugart Illo deceased August 7

2014 - Jeanette Dunton Gifford deceased August 19

PHOTOS

Photos

Made in the USA
Columbia, SC
22 December 2017